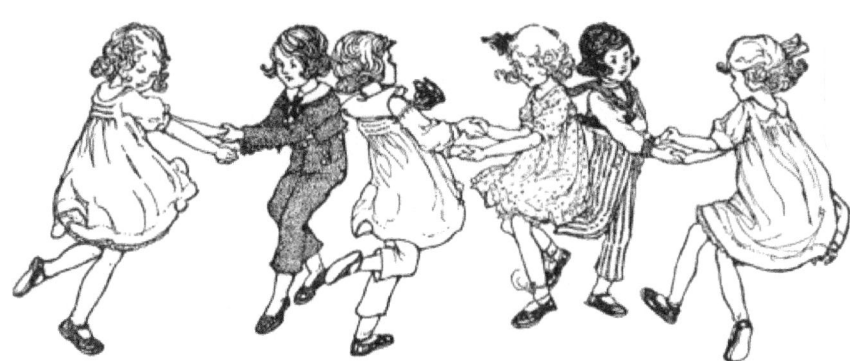

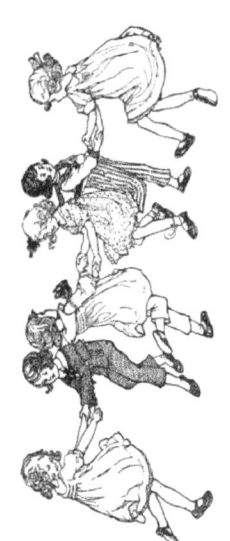

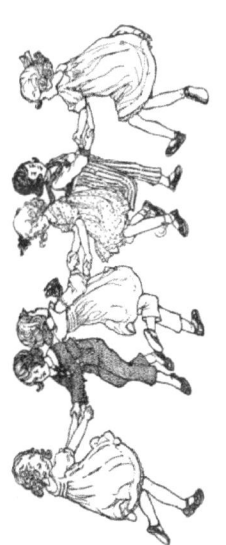

SWEET WHIMSY
VINTAGE CHILDREN
40 GRAYSCALE IMAGES

by *janet w long*

THIS BOOK BELONGS TO:

_____

START_____

FINISH_____

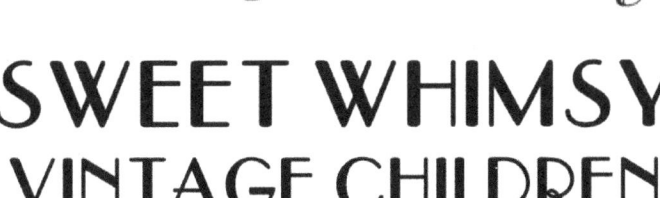

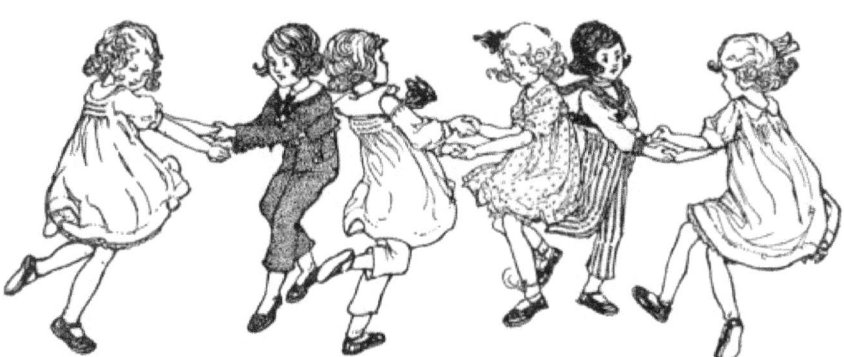

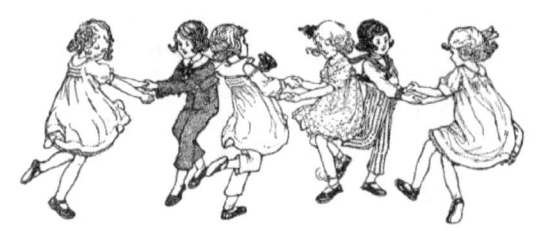

AMAZON AUTHOR PAGE:

https://www.amazon.com/author/janetlong

ETSY VINTAGE SHOP

"Go green! Buy vintage!"
https://www.etsy.com/il-en/shop/AdoptionsLtd

ETSY "JLA" SHOP

https://www.etsy.com/shop/JanetLongArts

[Photography & Watercolor prints, Hand Knits]

This book was developed by Janet W. Long in February 2017.

The images are from the public domain.

[Contact me if you find any images that are NOT in the public domain.]
EMAIL unrise@hotmail.com

ISBN-13: 978-1543197709   ISBN-10: 1543197701

SWEET WHIMSY
VINTAGE CHILDREN
40 GRAYSCALE IMAGES

INTRO...

I've chosen some adorable vintage children portrayed in photographs from the public domain for this book. It almost goes without saying that very old photographs have their own charm. There are irregularities not found in present day photographs. Please bear with me regarding this fact.

Several of my images in this book are in the 'film noir' style, deep black & white. When coloring these images, I like to leave the blacks intact & color the lighter areas for a dramatic, eye-catching look.

In grayscale coloring, the shading is already there. EVERYONE CAN BE AN ARTIST! Just apply a layer of color & there's your picture! I have intentionally put some lighter grayscale images in this & my other books, so you can have a bit more artistic 'freedom' to add your ideas.

There are blank pages at the back for your notes & coloring tool testing. The publisher has only one paper choice. I feel that it's a bit thin. But, that can be a **strength** when you are able to get a beautiful picture without having to do many layers or use too much pressure.

Discover how your various pencils or crayons interact to create the colors you love. You don't have to buy all the coloring tools & colors out there. You'll see that even if you have only ONE red pencil, you can create many shades of red by using a blue, orange, purple underlay/overlay. Use as many layers as you wish. YOU ARE THE COLORIST!

If you choose gel pens, felt tips, or other more 'liquid' mediums, please put a piece of cardstock or other paper behind your color work to catch any possible bleed through. You may want to cut out the pages to get a more open space to color. Go ahead, frame your work! Put it on your walls or give as a gift. It's ART!!

**THANK YOU Angelia Miller, Michelle Pillon
& Dena Mueller for coloring the cover art.**

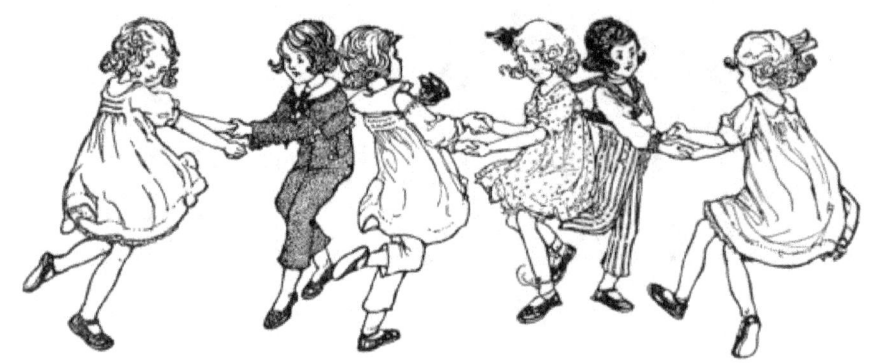

FIND ME

AMAZON AUTHOR PAGE: www.amazon.com/author/janetlong
ETSY SHOP, "JLA" www.janetlongarts/shop/Etsy.com
ETSY VINTAGE SHOP: www.etsy.com/shop/AdoptionsLtd

ETSY "JLA" RETAIL SHOP ON FACEBOOK:
www.facebook.com/Janet-Long-Arts- 192517394097105/
ETSY VINTAGE RETAIL SHOP on FACEBOOK: http://bit.ly/2iS45YC
TWITTER: twitter.com/jan43q
PINTEREST: pinterest.com/janetlongarts/
LINKEDIN: www.linkedin.com/profile/view?...

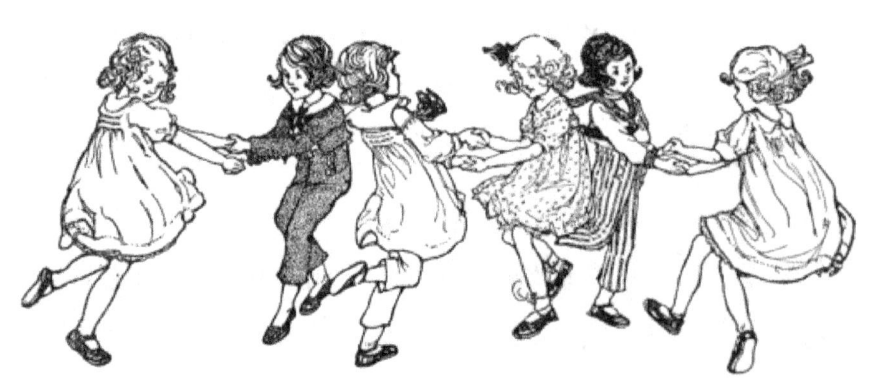

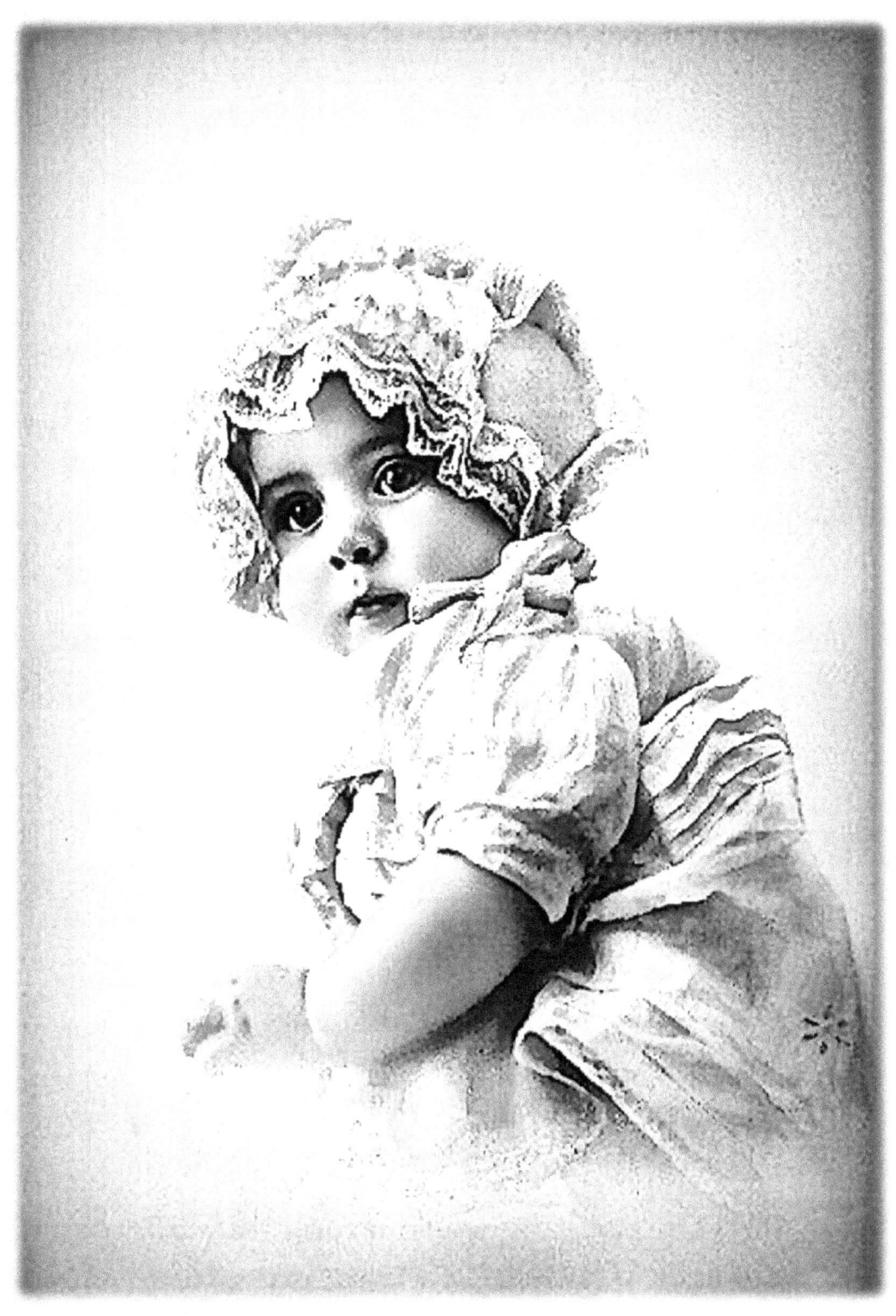

HELLO!

HELLO!

AMAZON AUTHOR PAGE: www.amazon.com/author/janetlong
ETSY SHOP, "JLA" www.janetlongarts/shop/Etsy.com
ETSY VINTAGE SHOP: www.etsy.com/shop/ AdoptionsLtd

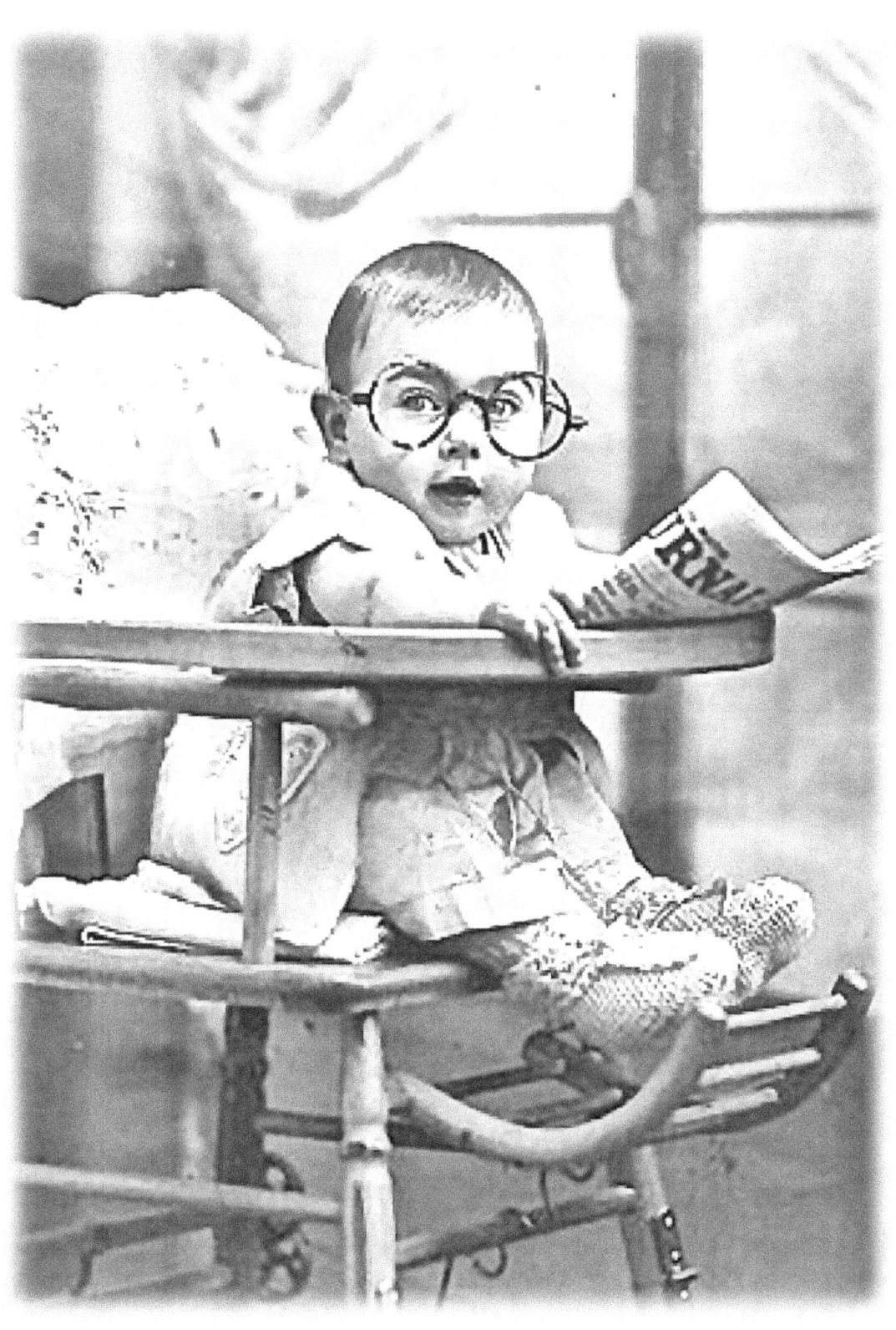

MARKET'S UP!

MARKET'S UP!
AMAZON AUTHOR PAGE: www.amazon.com/author/janetlong
ETSY SHOP, "JLA" www.janetlongarts/shop/Etsy.com
ETSY VINTAGE SHOP: www.etsy.com/shop/AdoptionsLtd

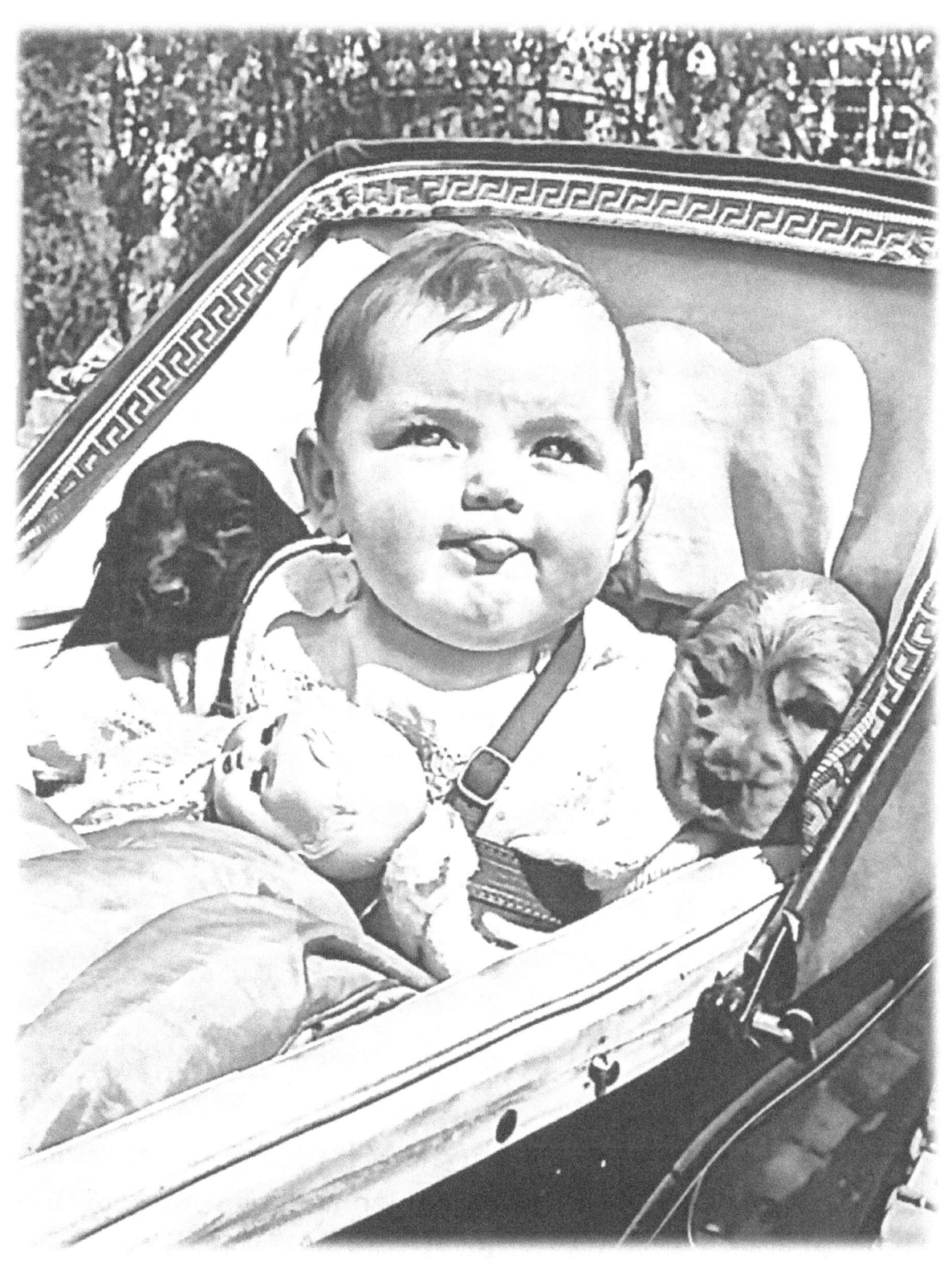

I LOVE LICKING MY DOGS!

I LOVE LICKING MY DOGS!
AMAZON AUTHOR PAGE: www.amazon.com/author/janetlong
ETSY SHOP, "JLA" www.janetlongarts/shop/Etsy.com
ETSY VINTAGE SHOP: www.etsy.com/shop/ AdoptionsLtd

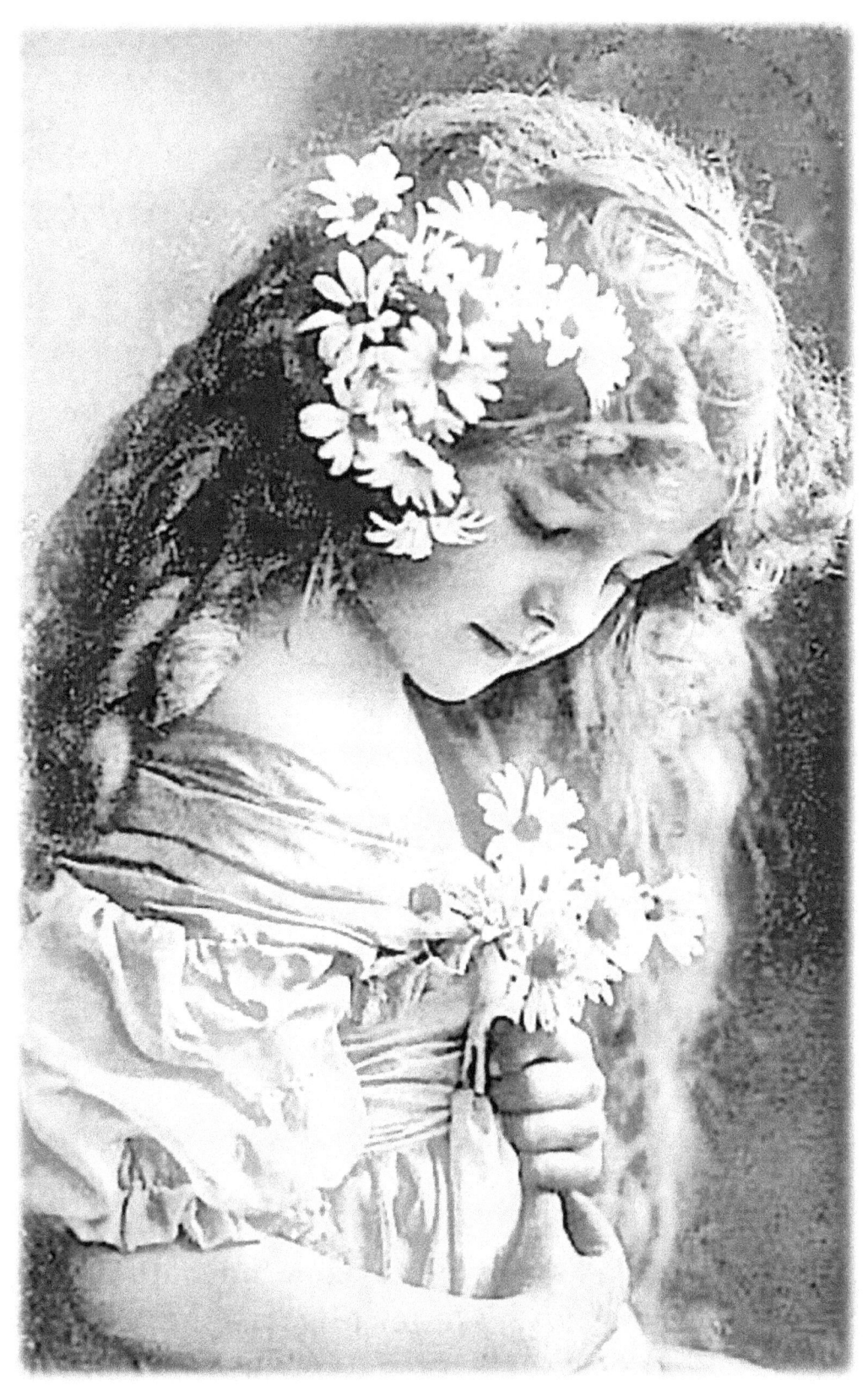

FLOWER GIRL

FLOWER GIRL

AMAZON AUTHOR PAGE: www.amazon.com/author/janetlong
ETSY SHOP, "JLA" www.janetlongarts/shop/Etsy.com
ETSY VINTAGE SHOP: www.etsy.com/shop/AdoptionsLtd

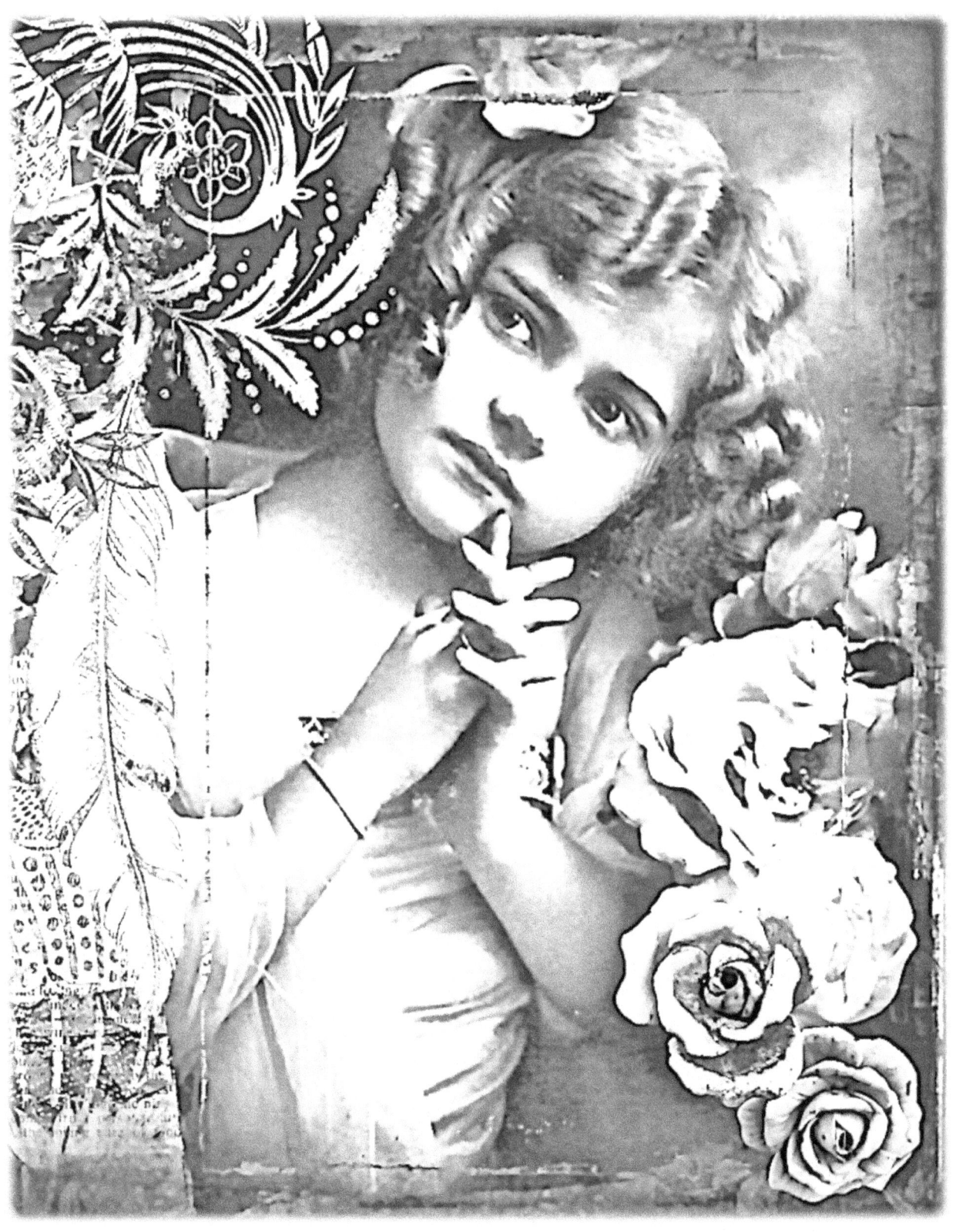

PENSIVE

PENSIVE?

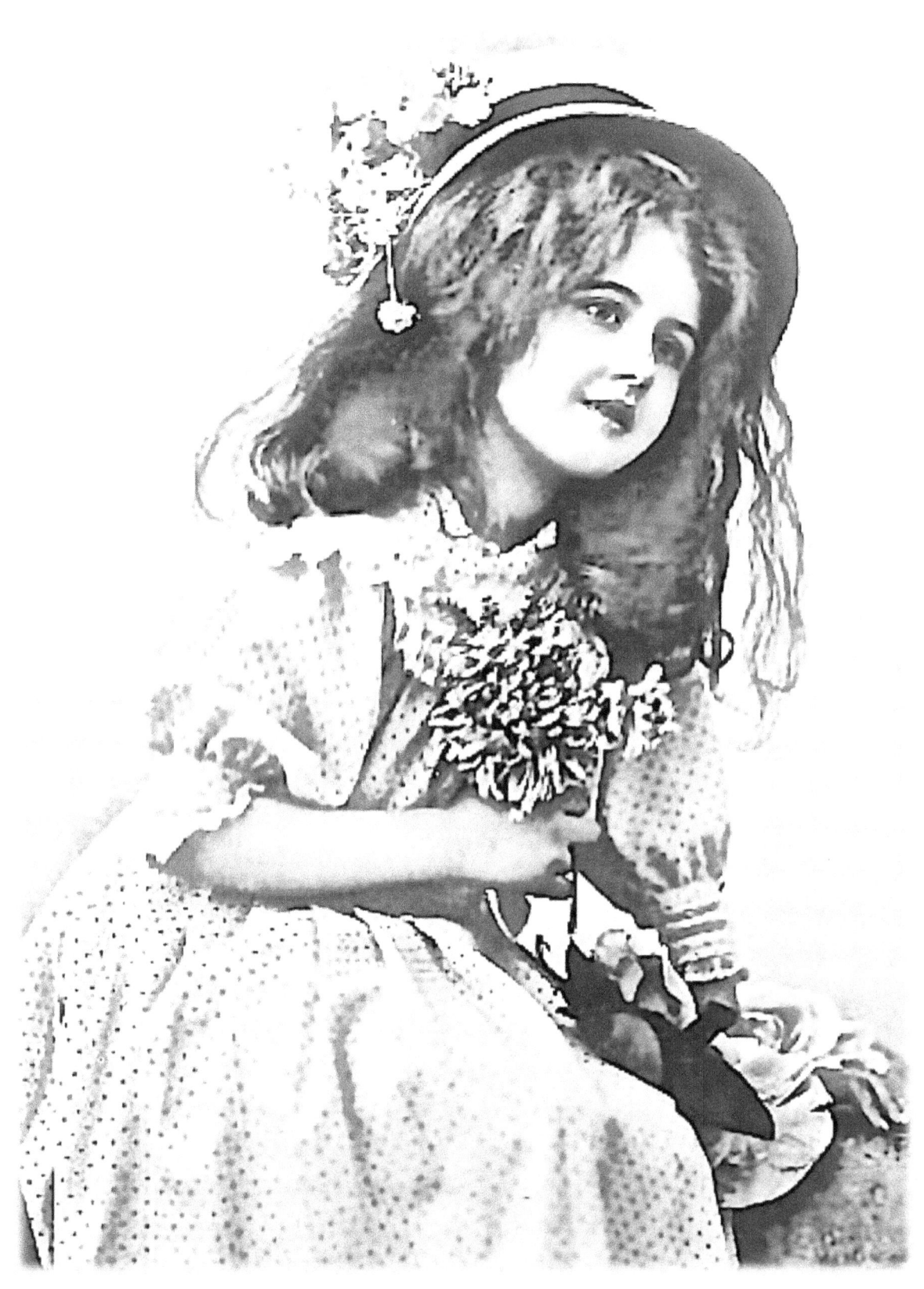

GOING TO GRANDMA'S HOUSE

GOING TO GRANDMA'S HOUSE
AMAZON AUTHOR PAGE: www.amazon.com/author/janetlong
ETSY SHOP, "JLA" www.janetlongarts/shop/Etsy.com
ETSY VINTAGE SHOP: www.etsy.com/shop/AdoptionsLtd

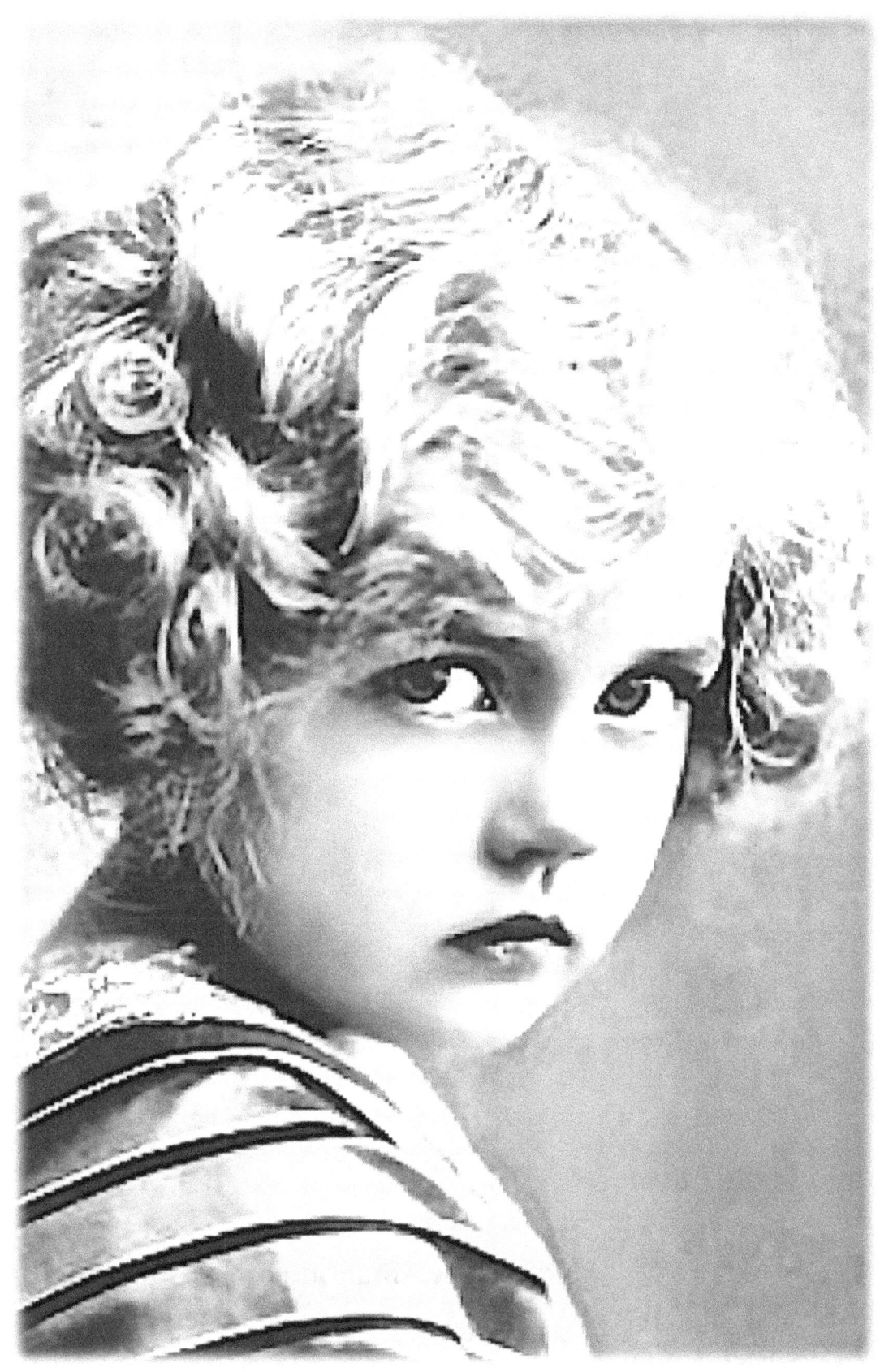

AMAZON AUTHOR PAGE: www.amazon.com/author/janetlong
ETSY SHOP, "JLA" www.janetlongarts/shop/Etsy.com
ETSY VINTAGE SHOP: www.etsy.com/shop/AdoptionsLtd

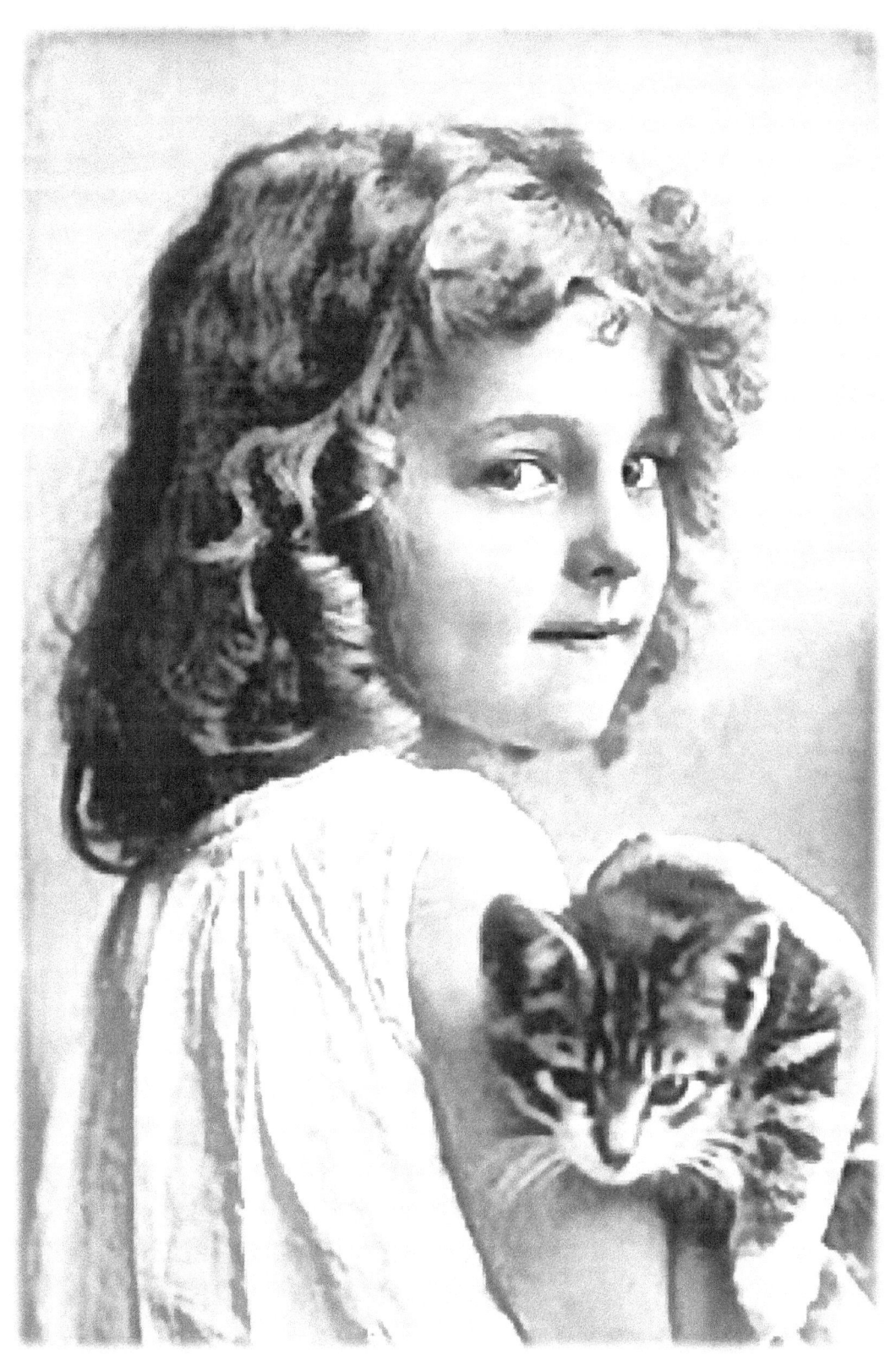

GRETE REINWALD 1902- 1983 & HER CAT!!

GRETE REINWALD 1902- 1983 & HER CAT!!
AMAZON AUTHOR PAGE: www.amazon.com/author/janetlong
ETSY SHOP, "JLA" www.janetlongarts/shop/Etsy.com
ETSY VINTAGE SHOP: www.etsy.com/shop/ AdoptionsLtd

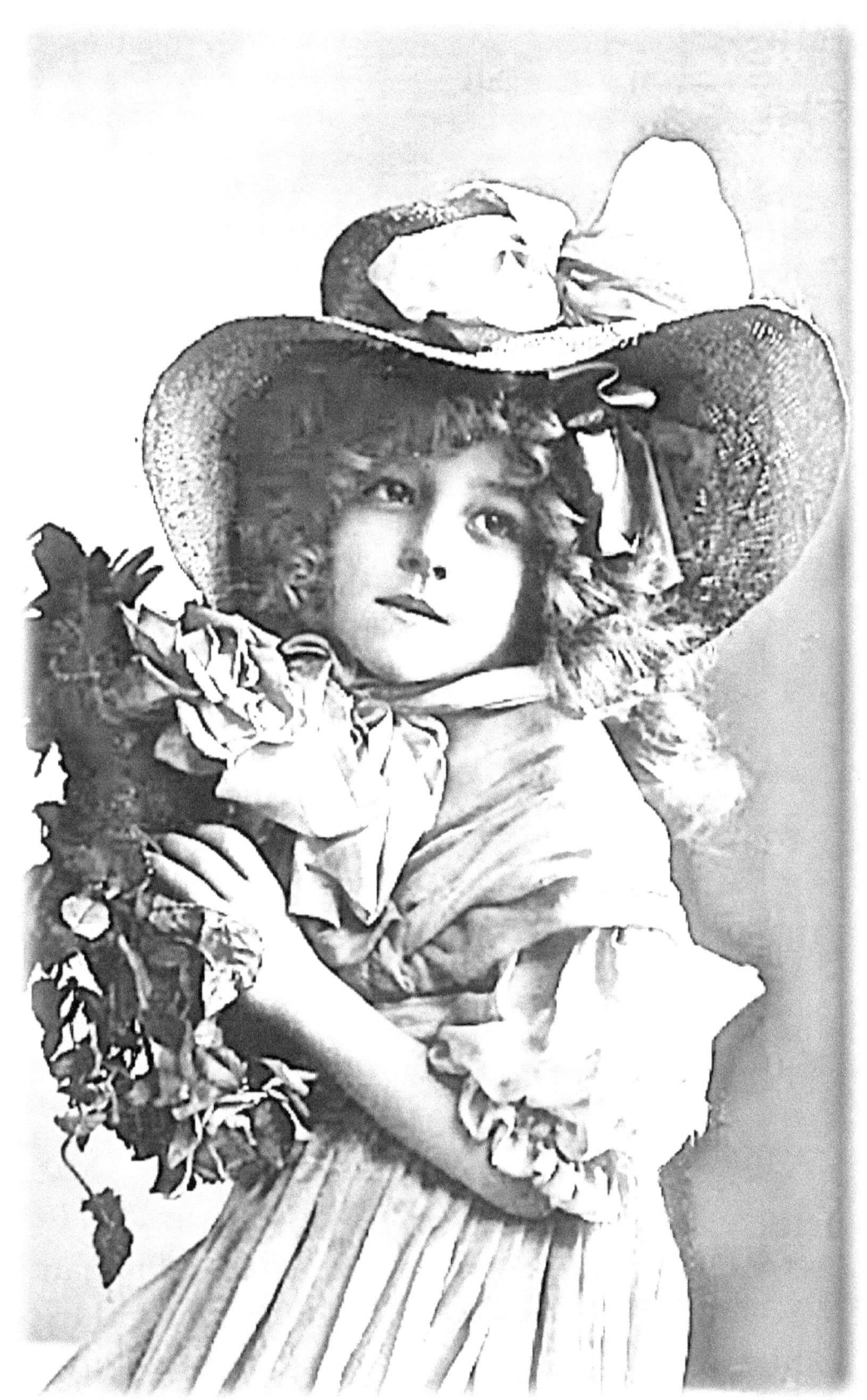

GRETE REINWALD 1902-1983

GRETE REINWALD 1902-1983
AMAZON AUTHOR PAGE: www.amazon.com/author/janetlong
ETSY SHOP, "JLA" www.janetlongarts/shop/Etsy.com
ETSY VINTAGE SHOP: www.etsy.com/shop/AdoptionsLtd

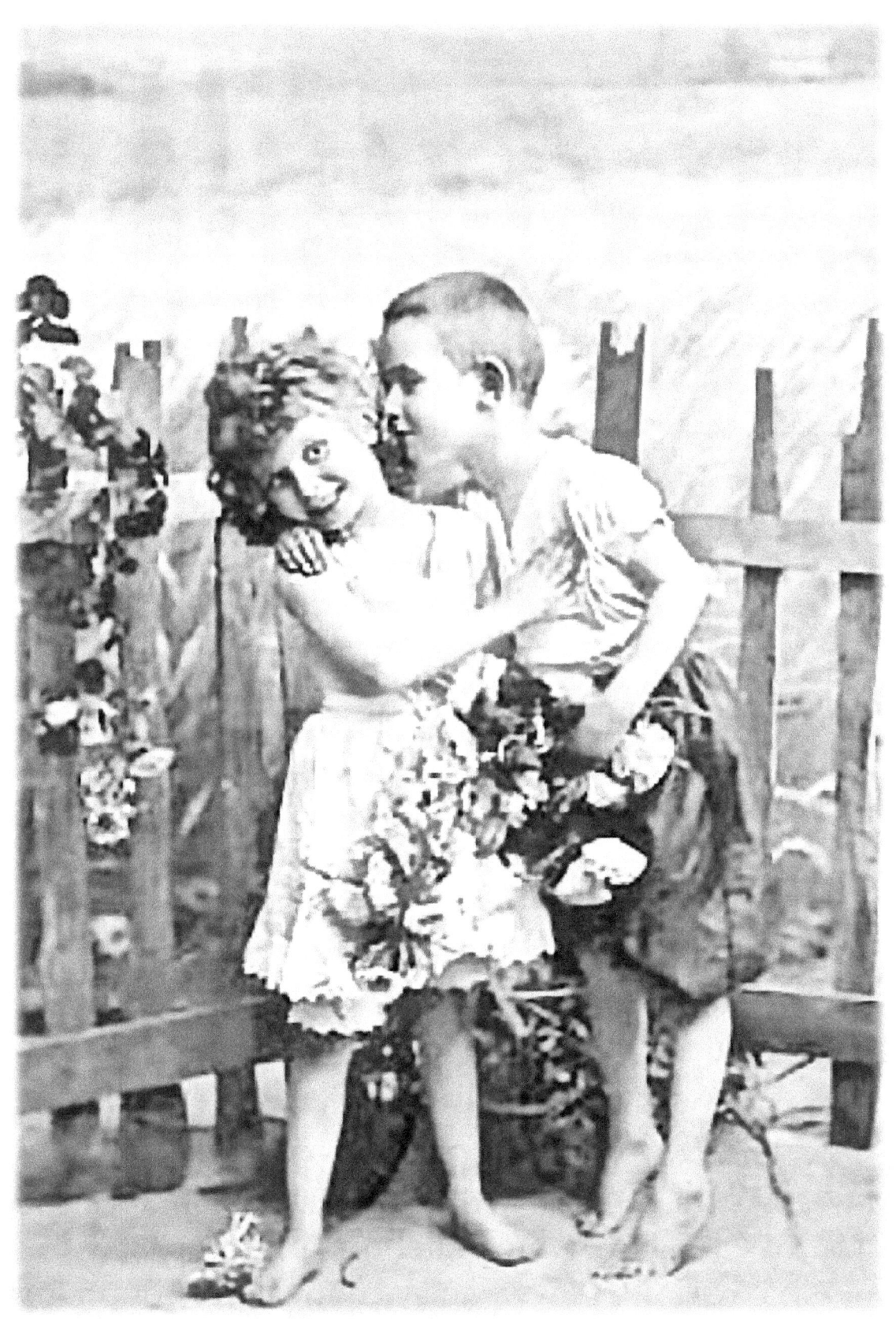

EYE ROLL ROMANCE?

EYE ROLL ROMANCE?
AMAZON AUTHOR PAGE: www.amazon.com/author/janetlong
ETSY SHOP, "JLA" www.janetlongarts/shop/Etsy.com
ETSY VINTAGE SHOP: www.etsy.com/shop/AdoptionsLtd

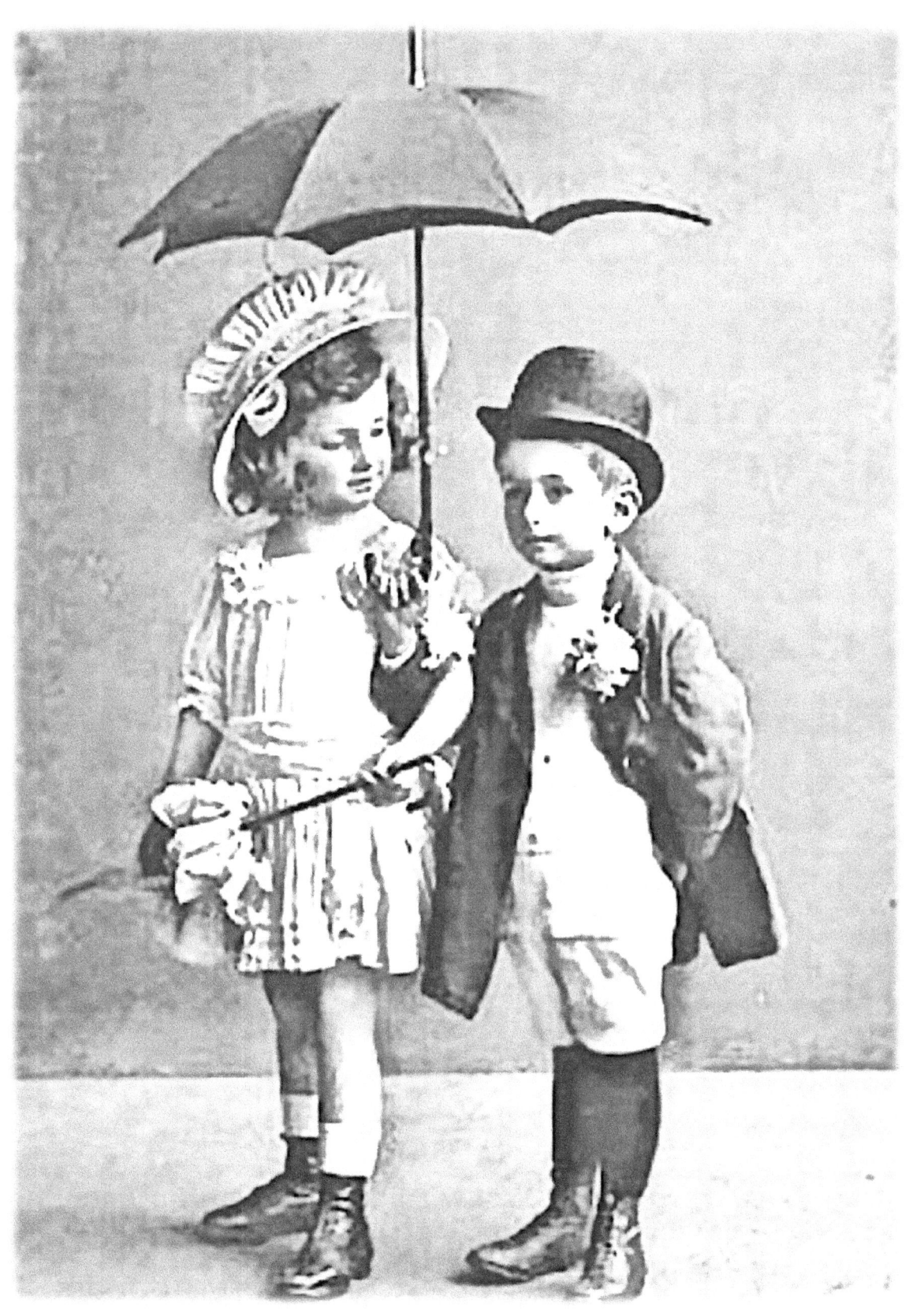

RAINY DAY ROMANCE?

RAINY DAY ROMANCE?
AMAZON AUTHOR PAGE: www.amazon.com/author/janetlong
ETSY SHOP, "JLA" www.janetlongarts/shop/Etsy.com
ETSY VINTAGE SHOP: www.etsy.com/shop/AdoptionsLtd

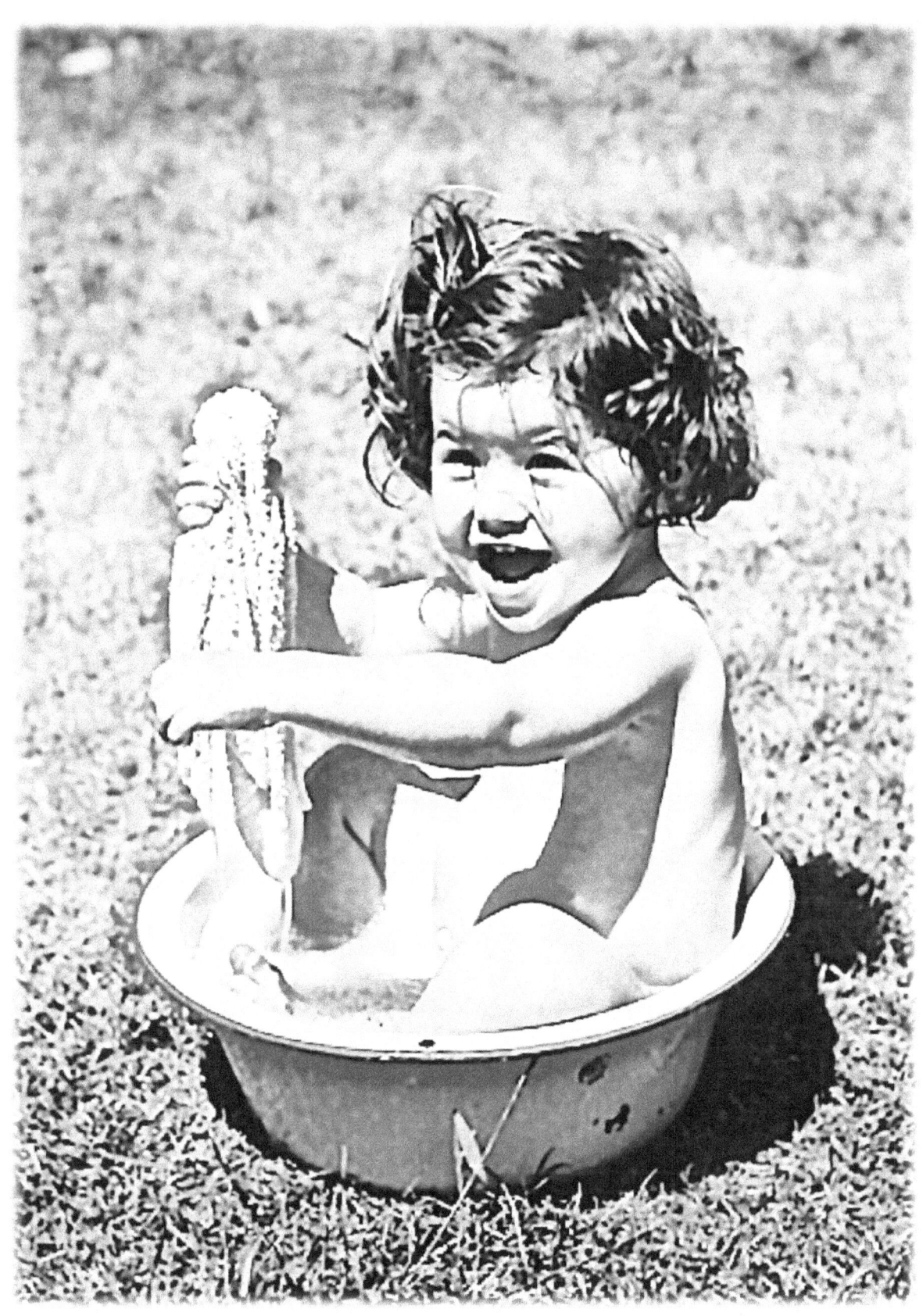

BATHTIME

BATHTIME

AMAZON AUTHOR PAGE: www.amazon.com/author/janetlong
ETSY SHOP, "JLA" www.janetlongarts/shop/Etsy.com
ETSY VINTAGE SHOP: www.etsy.com/shop/AdoptionsLtd

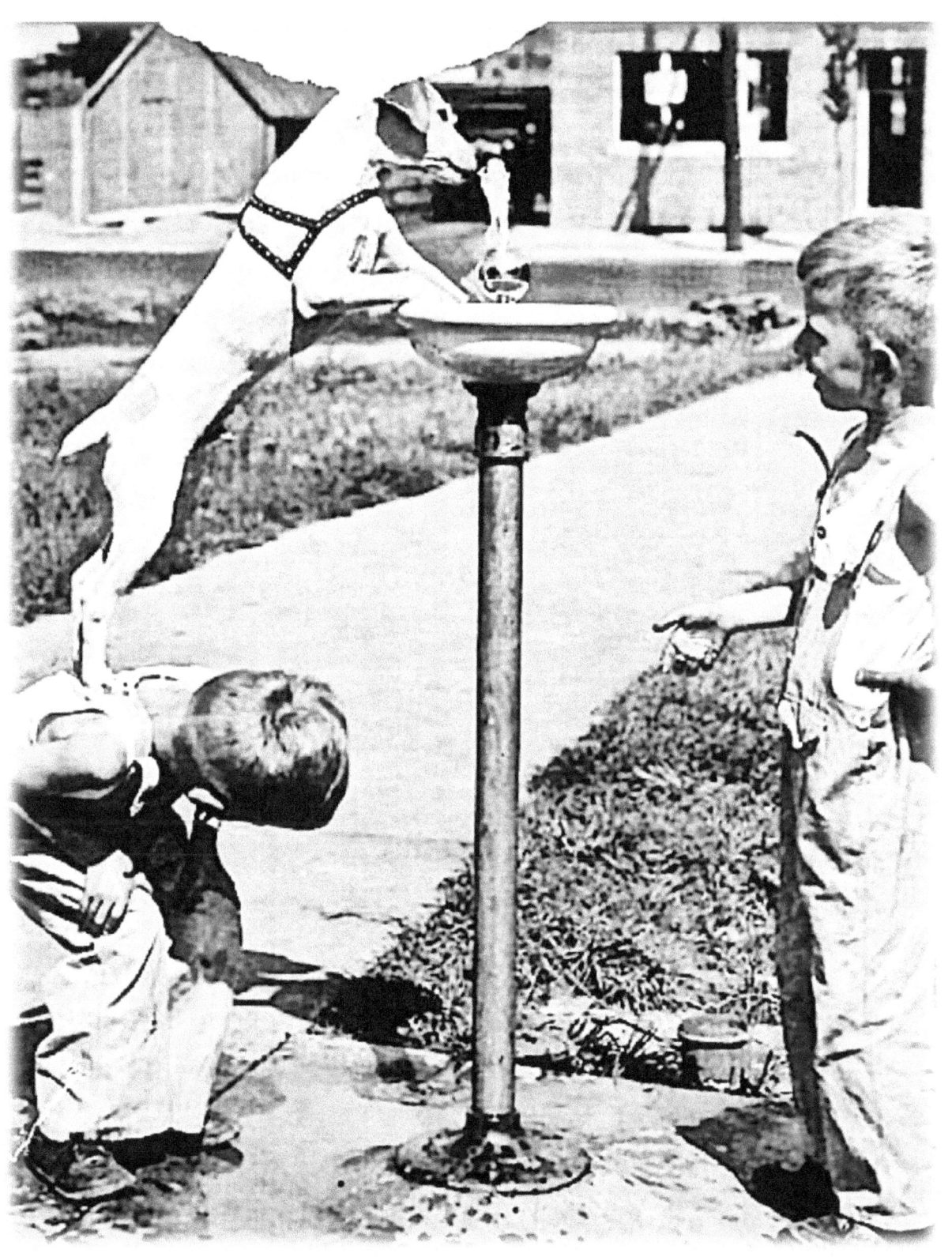

THIRSTY!

THIRSTY!
AMAZON AUTHOR PAGE: www.amazon.com/author/janetlong
ETSY SHOP, "JLA" www.janetlongarts/shop/Etsy.com
ETSY VINTAGE SHOP: www.etsy.com/shop/ AdoptionsLtd

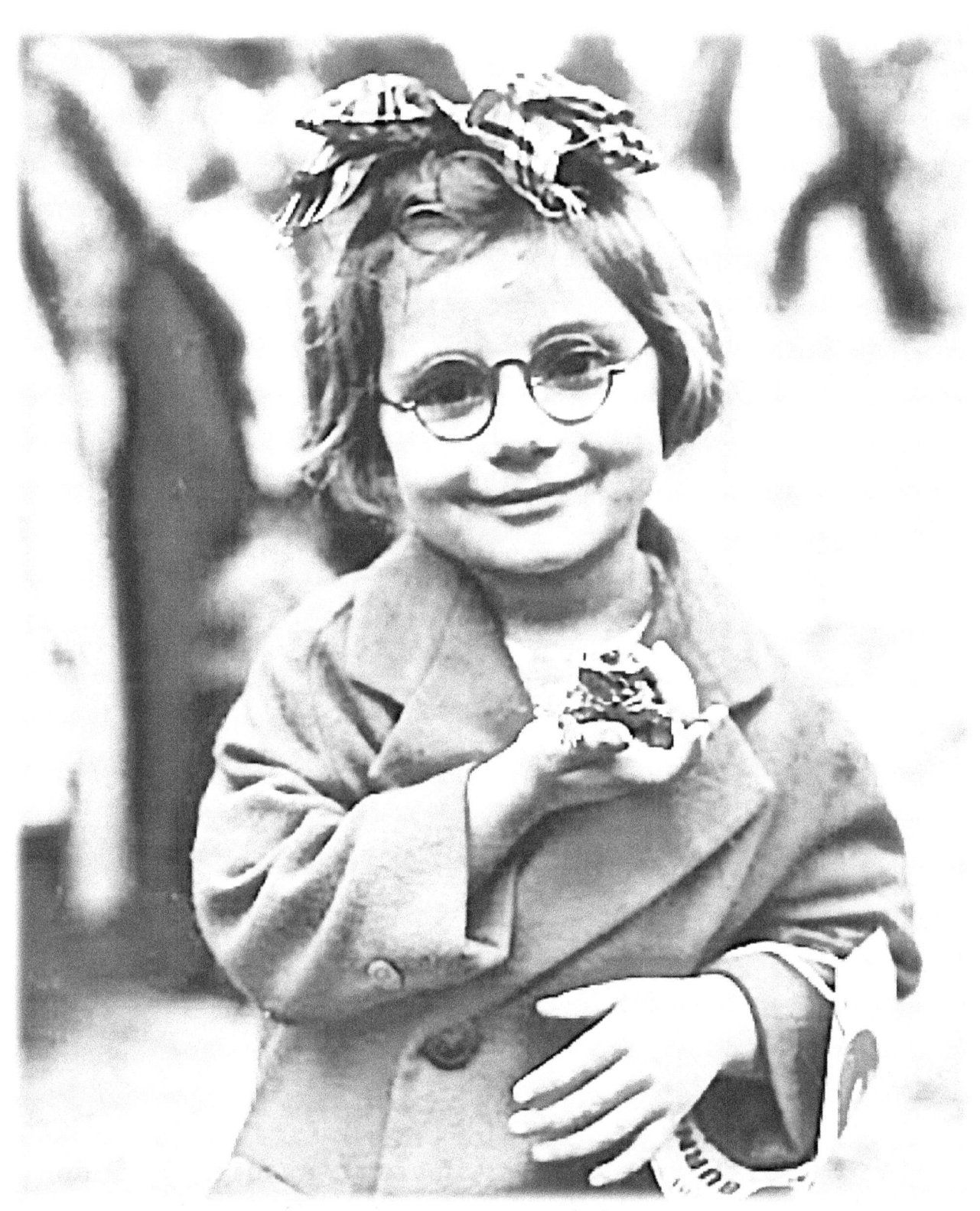

DO YOU LIKE MY FROG?

DO YOU LIKE MY FROG?
AMAZON AUTHOR PAGE: www.amazon.com/author/janetlong
ETSY SHOP, "JLA" www.janetlongarts/shop/Etsy.com
ETSY VINTAGE SHOP: www.etsy.com/shop/AdoptionsLtd

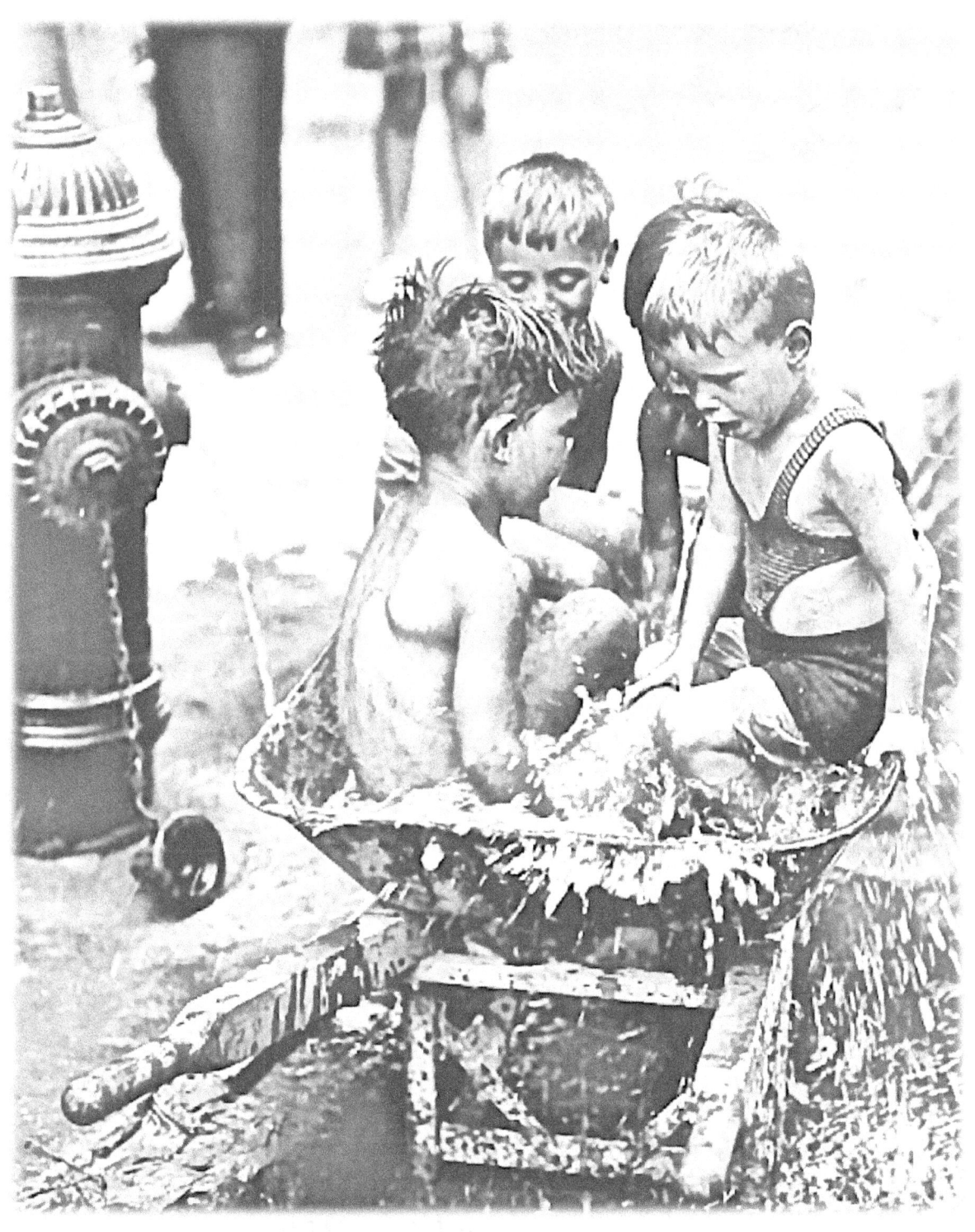

COOL POOL!

COOL POOL!
AMAZON AUTHOR PAGE: www.amazon.com/author/janetlong
ETSY SHOP, "JLA" www.janetlongarts/shop/Etsy.com
ETSY VINTAGE SHOP: www.etsy.com/shop/ AdoptionsLtd

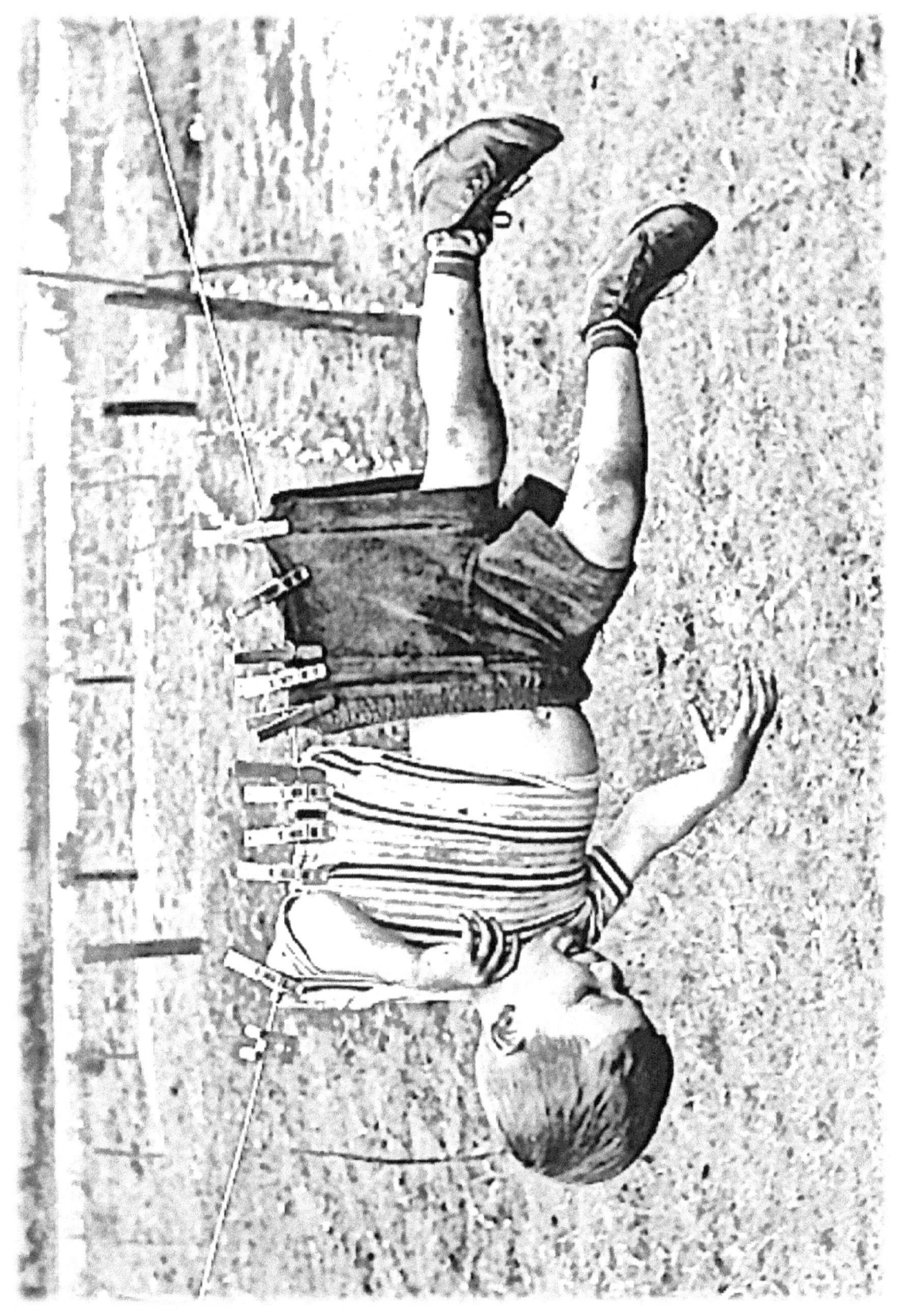

SHE HUNG ME OUT TO DRY!!

SHE HUNG ME OUT TO DRY!
AMAZON AUTHOR PAGE: www.amazon.com/author/janetlong
ETSY SHOP, "JLA" www.janetlongarts/shop/Etsy.com
ETSY VINTAGE SHOP: www.etsy.com/shop/AdoptionsLtd

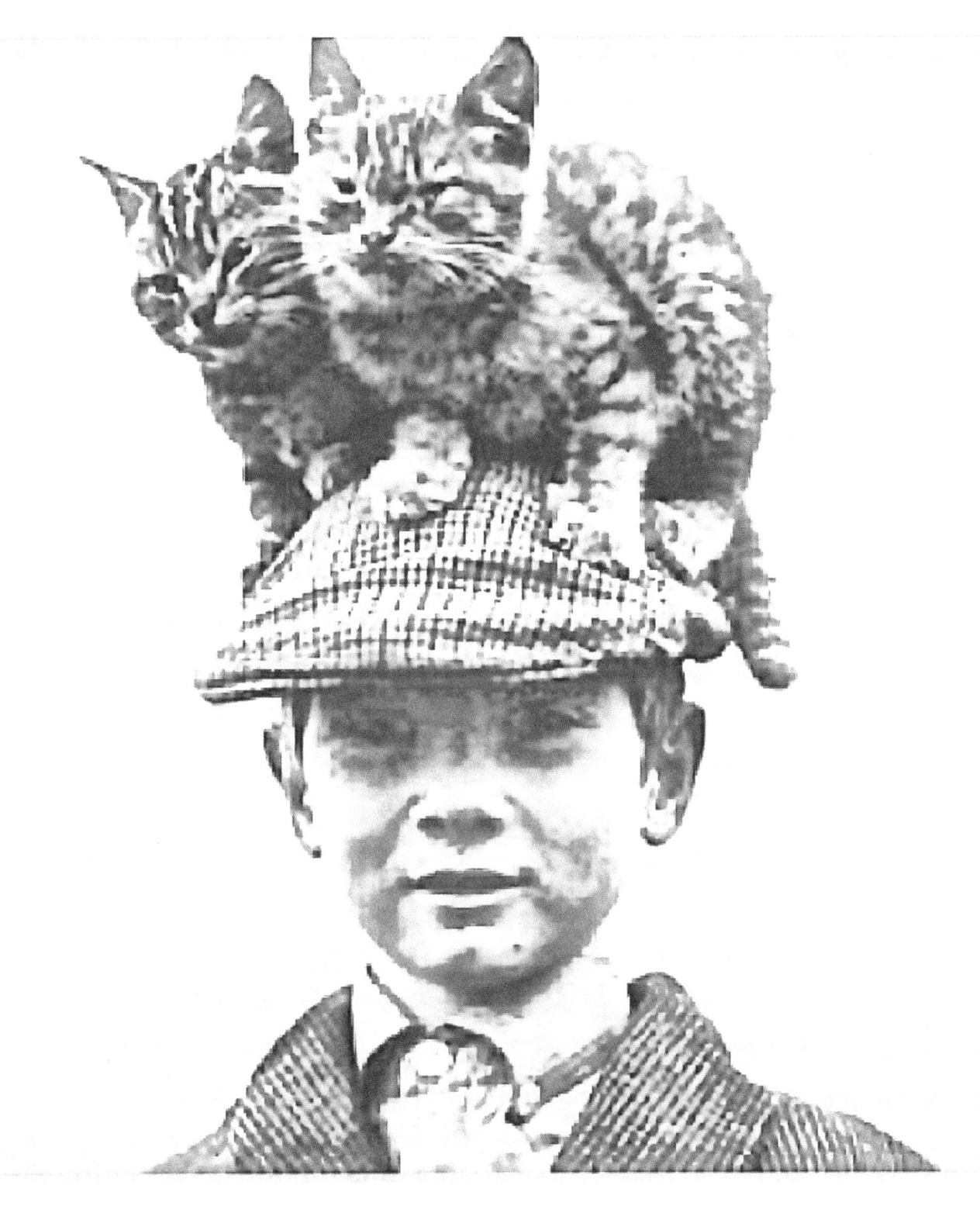

CATS ON the HAT

CATS ON the HAT

AMAZON AUTHOR PAGE: www.amazon.com/author/janetlong
ETSY SHOP, "JLA" www.janetlongarts/shop/Etsy.com
ETSY VINTAGE SHOP: www.etsy.com/shop/ AdoptionsLtd

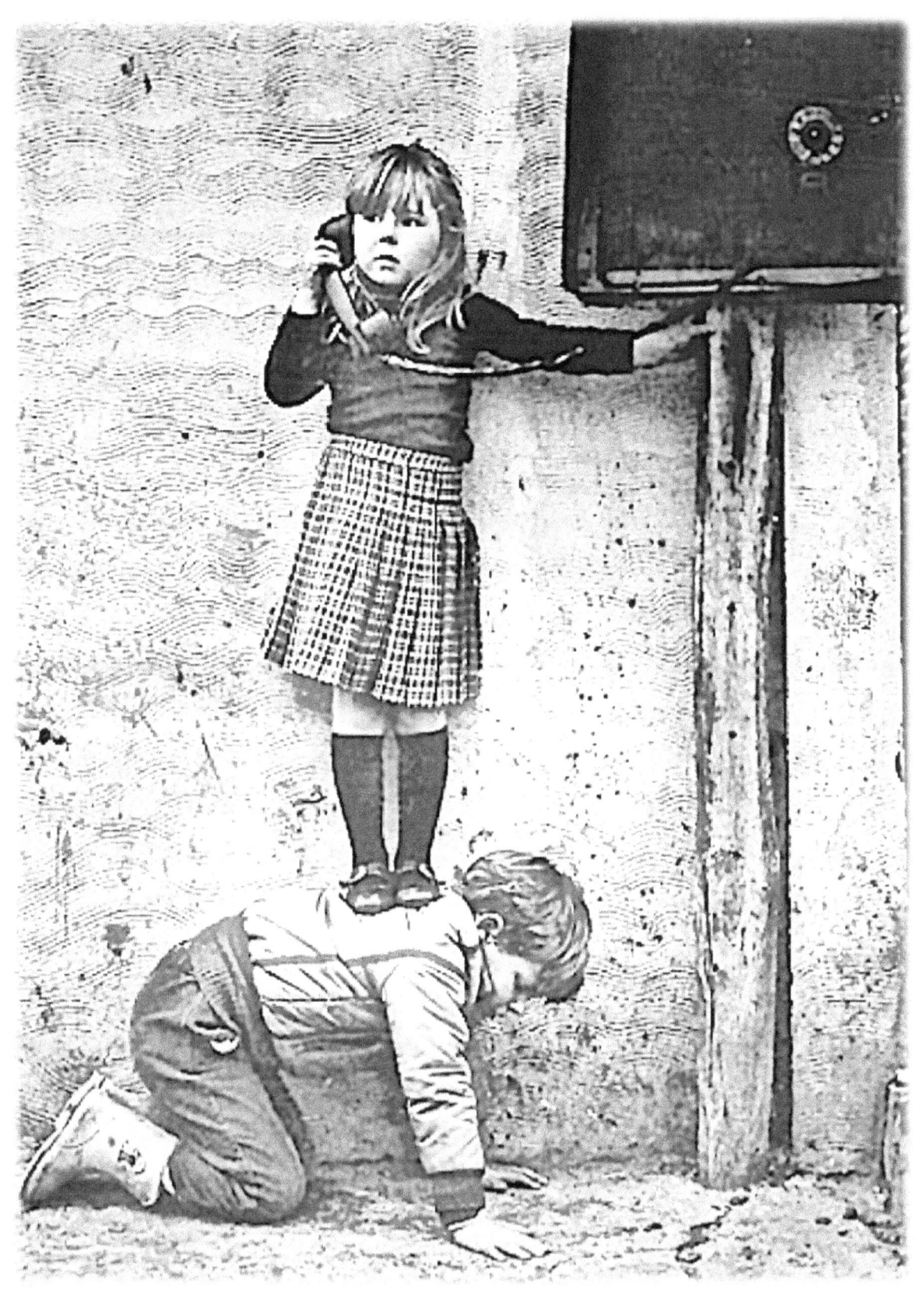

A HELPING HAND or ?!

A HELPING HAND or ?!
AMAZON AUTHOR PAGE: www.amazon.com/author/janetlong
ETSY SHOP, "JLA" www.janetlongarts/shop/Etsy.com
ETSY VINTAGE SHOP: www.etsy.com/shop/AdoptionsLtd

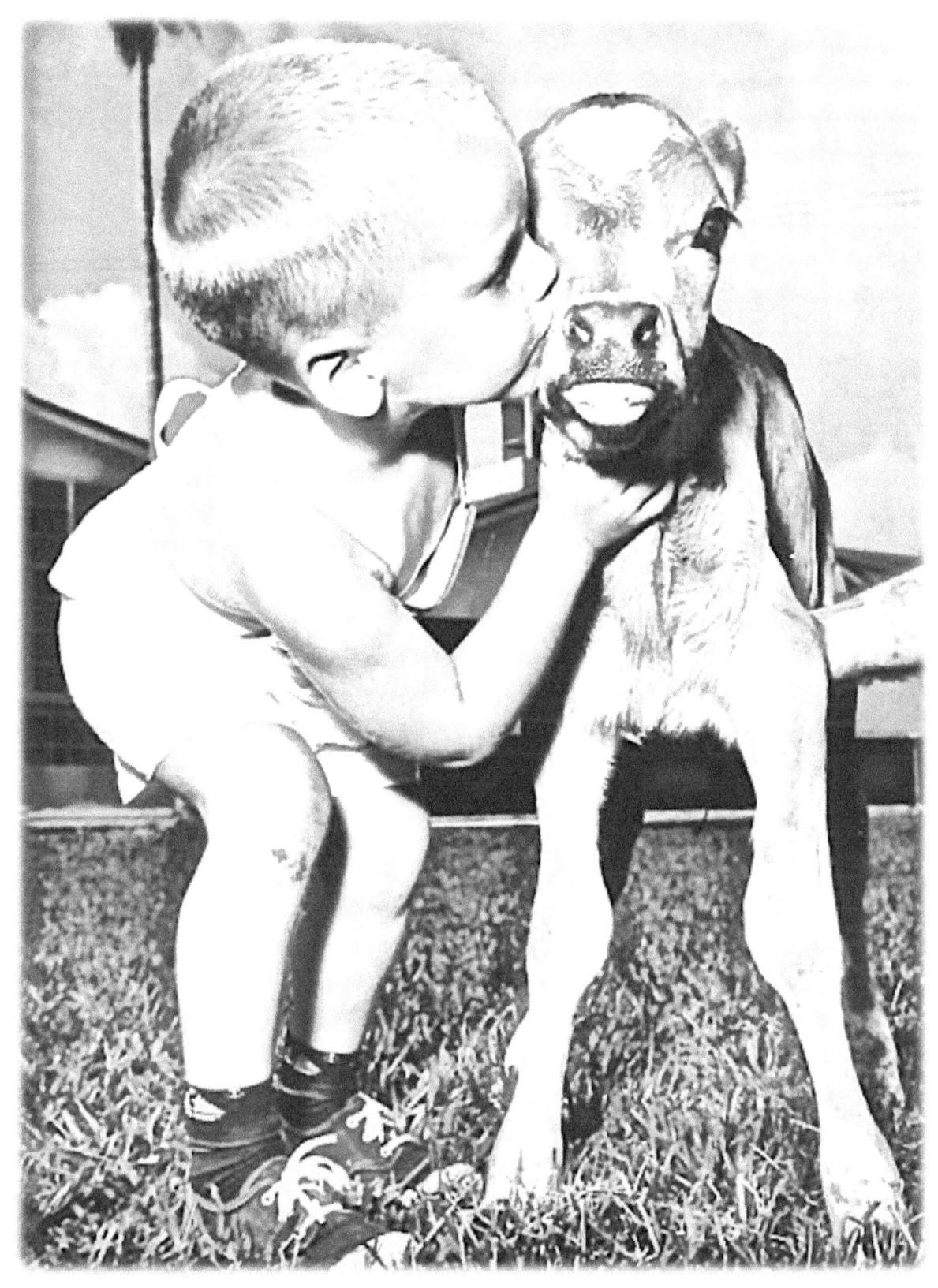

I LOVE MY BABY COW!

I LOVE MY COW!
AMAZON AUTHOR PAGE: www.amazon.com/author/janetlong
ETSY SHOP, "JLA" www.janetlongarts/shop/Etsy.com
ETSY VINTAGE SHOP: www.etsy.com/shop/AdoptionsLtd

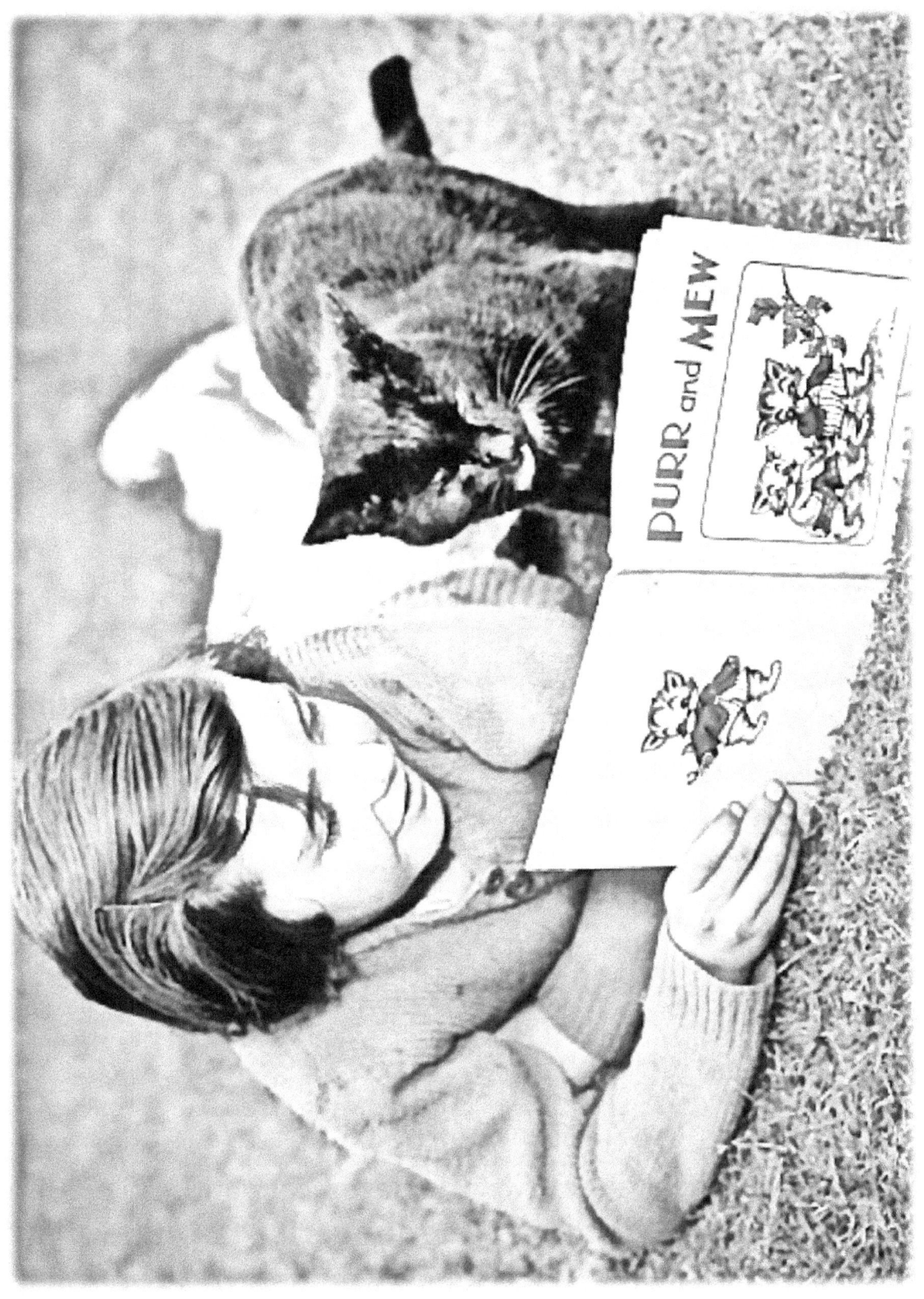

SHE LOVES THIS STORY!

SHE LOVES THIS STORY!
AMAZON AUTHOR PAGE: www.amazon.com/author/janetlong
ETSY SHOP, "JLA" www.janetlongarts/shop/Etsy.com
ETSY VINTAGE SHOP: www.etsy.com/shop/AdoptionsLtd

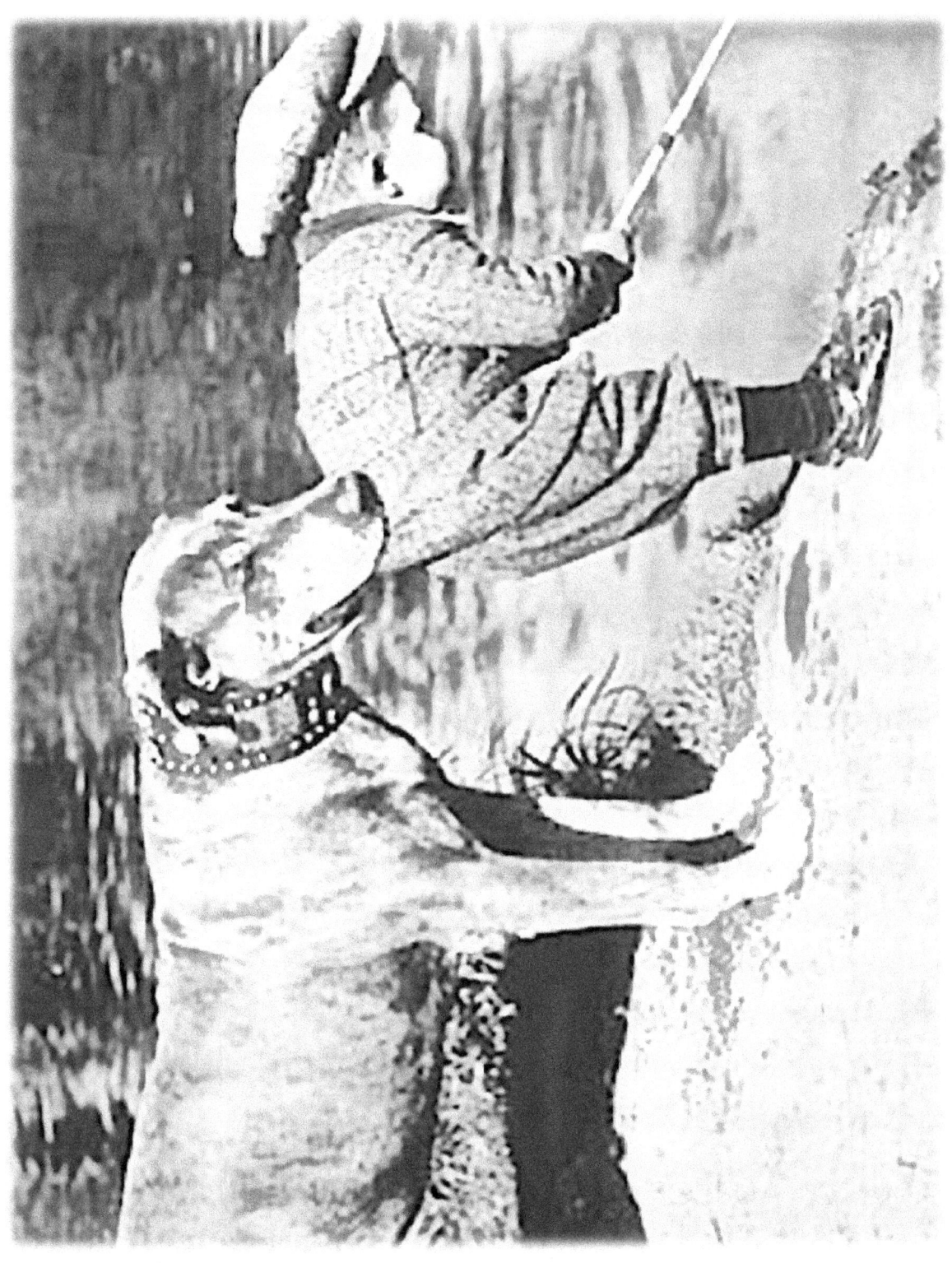

MY LIFEGUARD
AMAZON AUTHOR PAGE: www.amazon.com/author/janetlong
ETSY SHOP, "JLA" www.janetlongarts/shop/Etsy.com
ETSY VINTAGE SHOP: www.etsy.com/shop/AdoptionsLtd

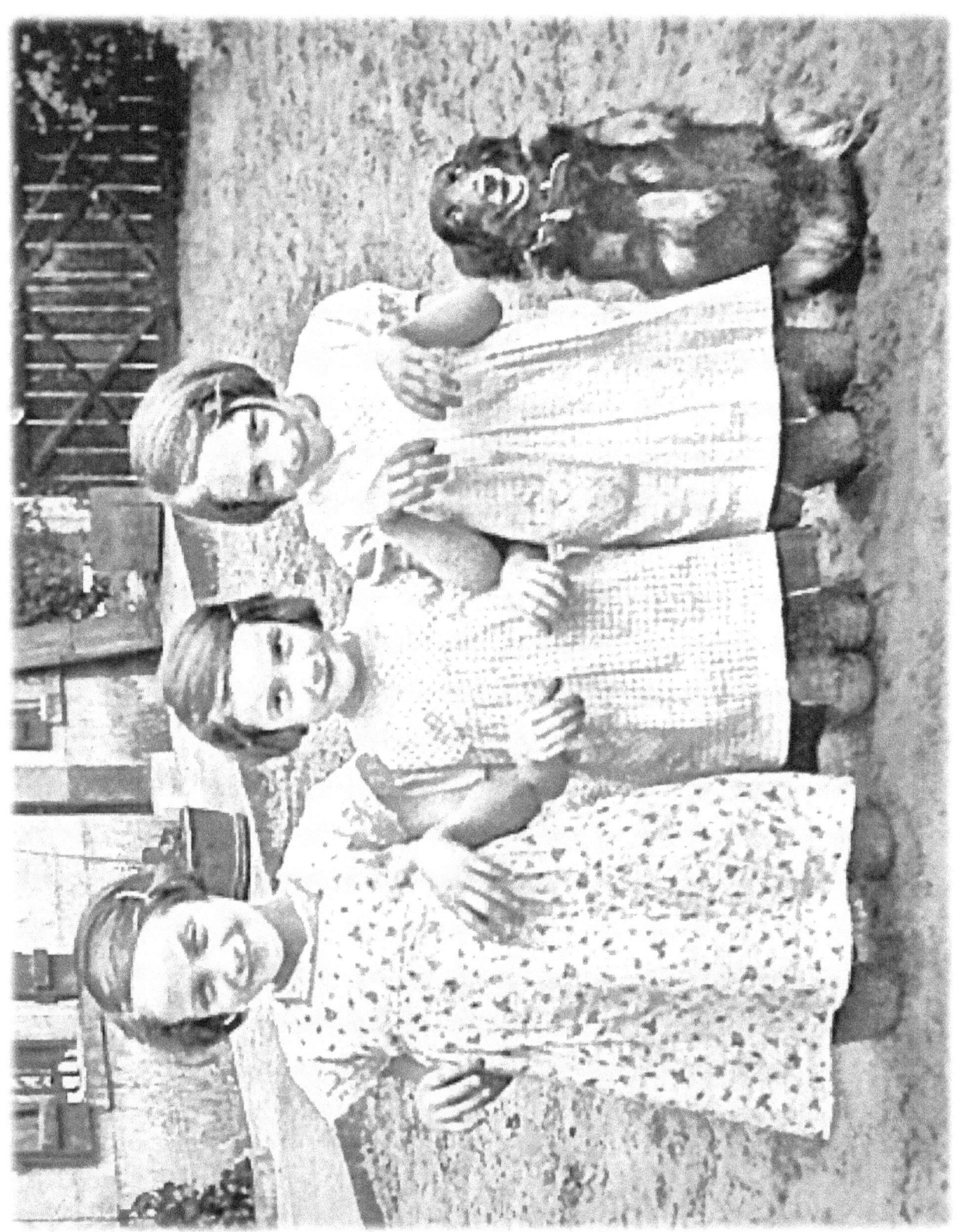

MONKEY SEE? MONKEY DO?
AMAZON AUTHOR PAGE: www.amazon.com/author/janetlong
ETSY SHOP, "JLA" www.janetlongarts/shop/Etsy.com
ETSY VINTAGE SHOP: www.etsy.com/shop/AdoptionsLtd

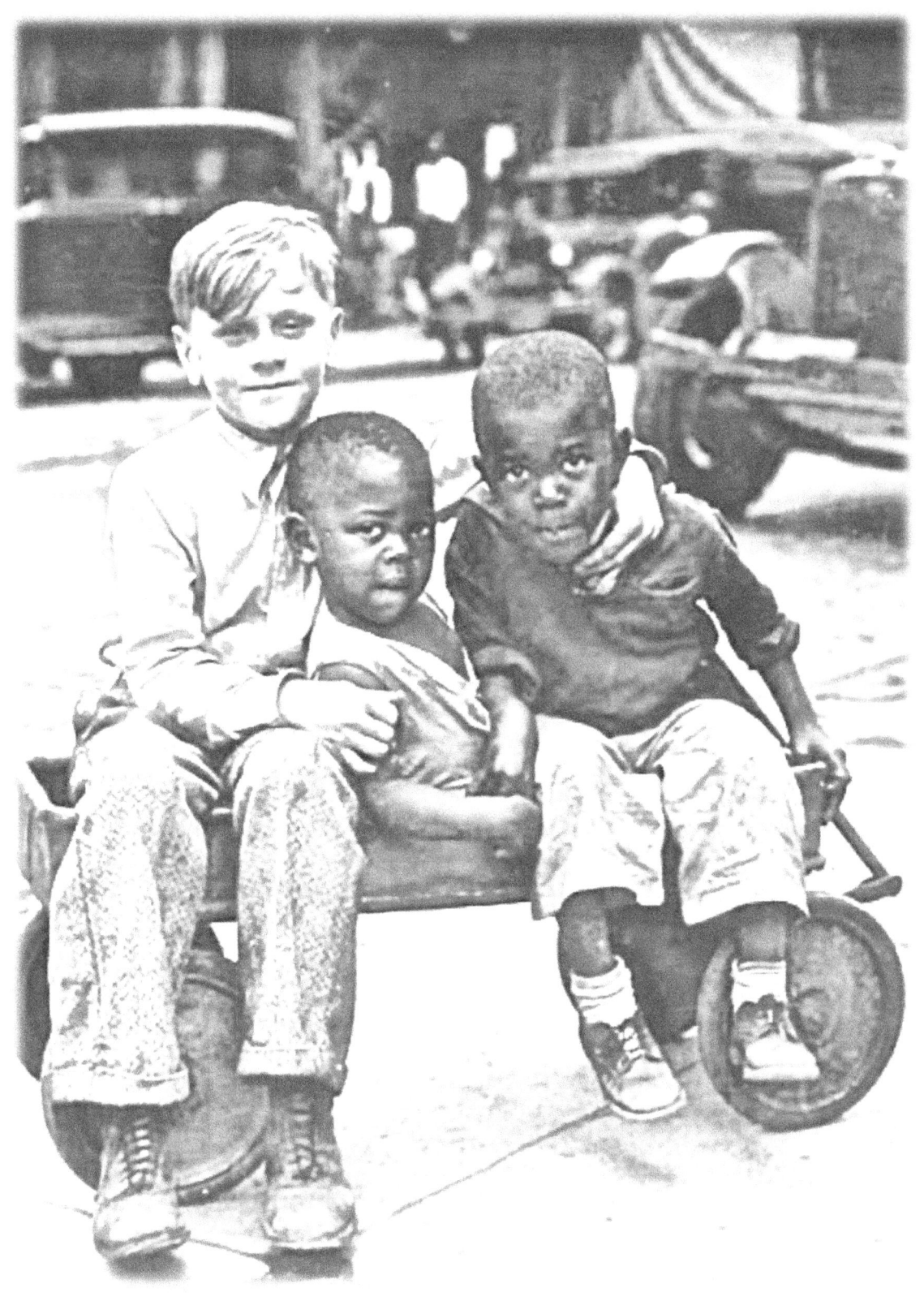

BFF'S

BFF'S
AMAZON AUTHOR PAGE: www.amazon.com/author/janetlong
ETSY SHOP, "JLA" www.janetlongarts/shop/Etsy.com
ETSY VINTAGE SHOP: www.etsy.com/shop/AdoptionsLtd

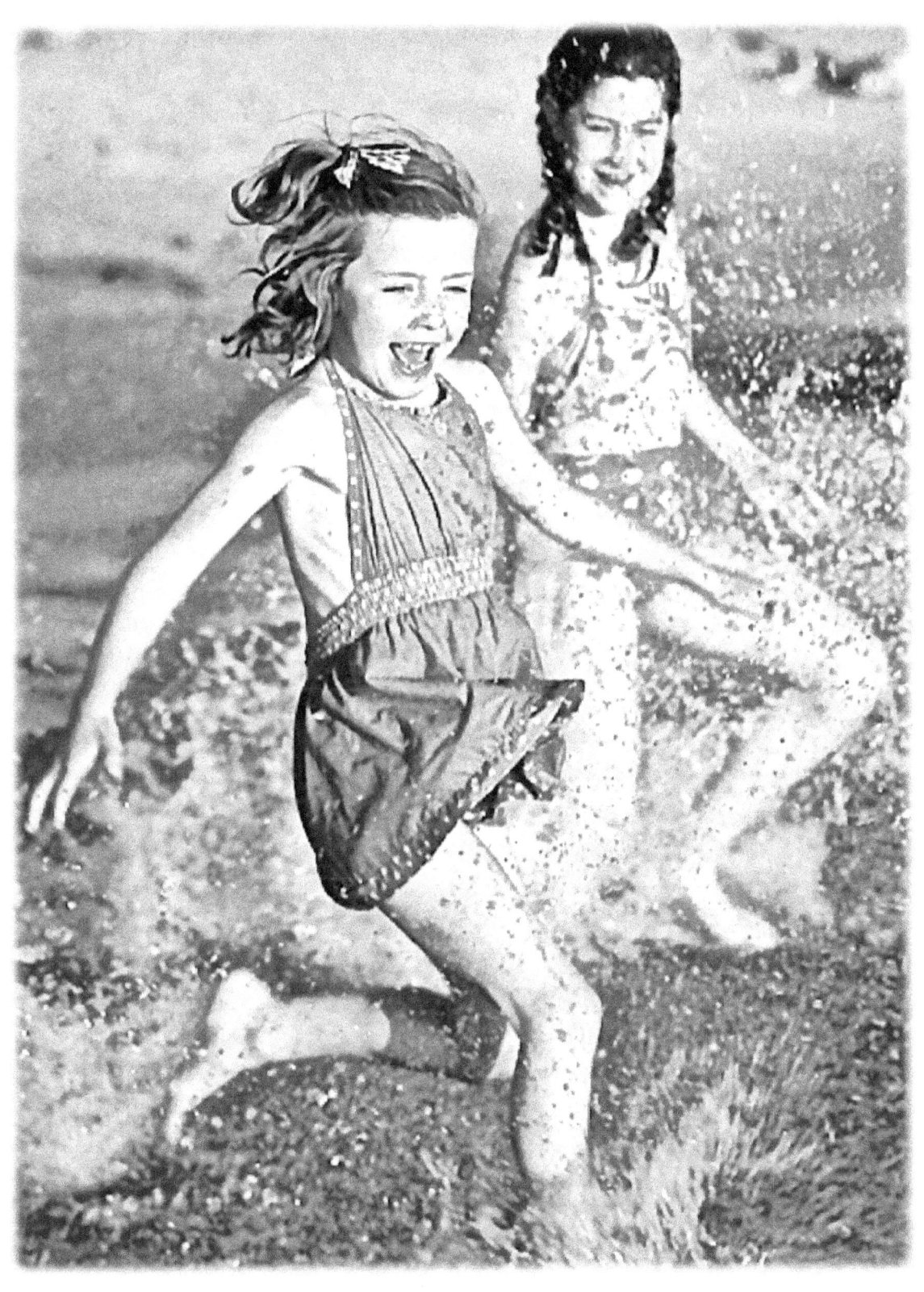

SPLISH SPLASH, I'M TAKIN' A BATH!

SPLISH SPLASH, I'M TAKIN' A BATH!
AMAZON AUTHOR PAGE: www.amazon.com/author/janetlong
ETSY SHOP, "JLA" www.janetlongarts/shop/Etsy.com
ETSY VINTAGE SHOP: www.etsy.com/shop/AdoptionsLtd

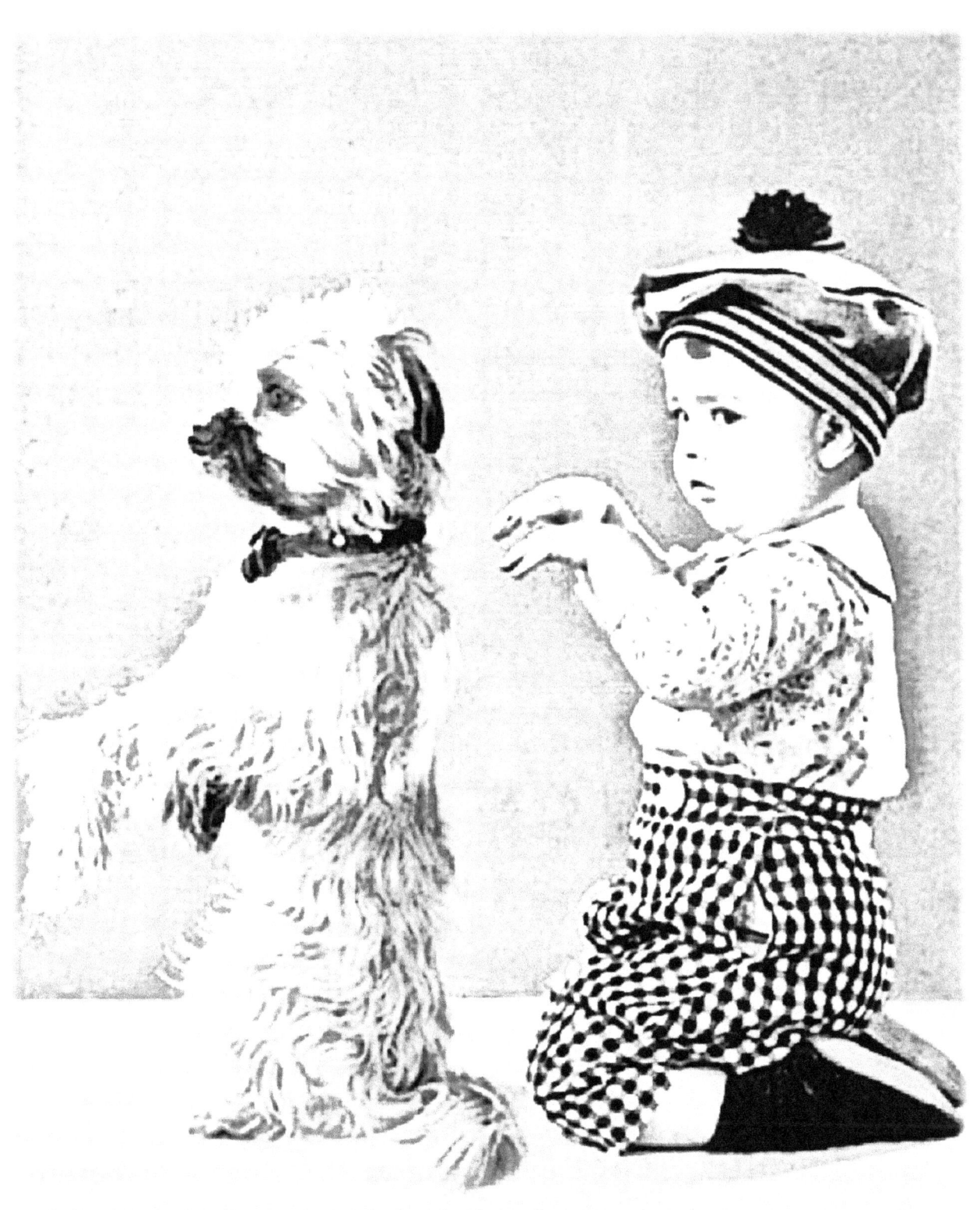

FOLLOW THE LEADER!

FOLLOW THE LEADER!
AMAZON AUTHOR PAGE: www.amazon.com/author/janetlong
ETSY SHOP, "JLA" www.janetlongarts/shop/Etsy.com
ETSY VINTAGE SHOP: www.etsy.com/shop/AdoptionsLtd

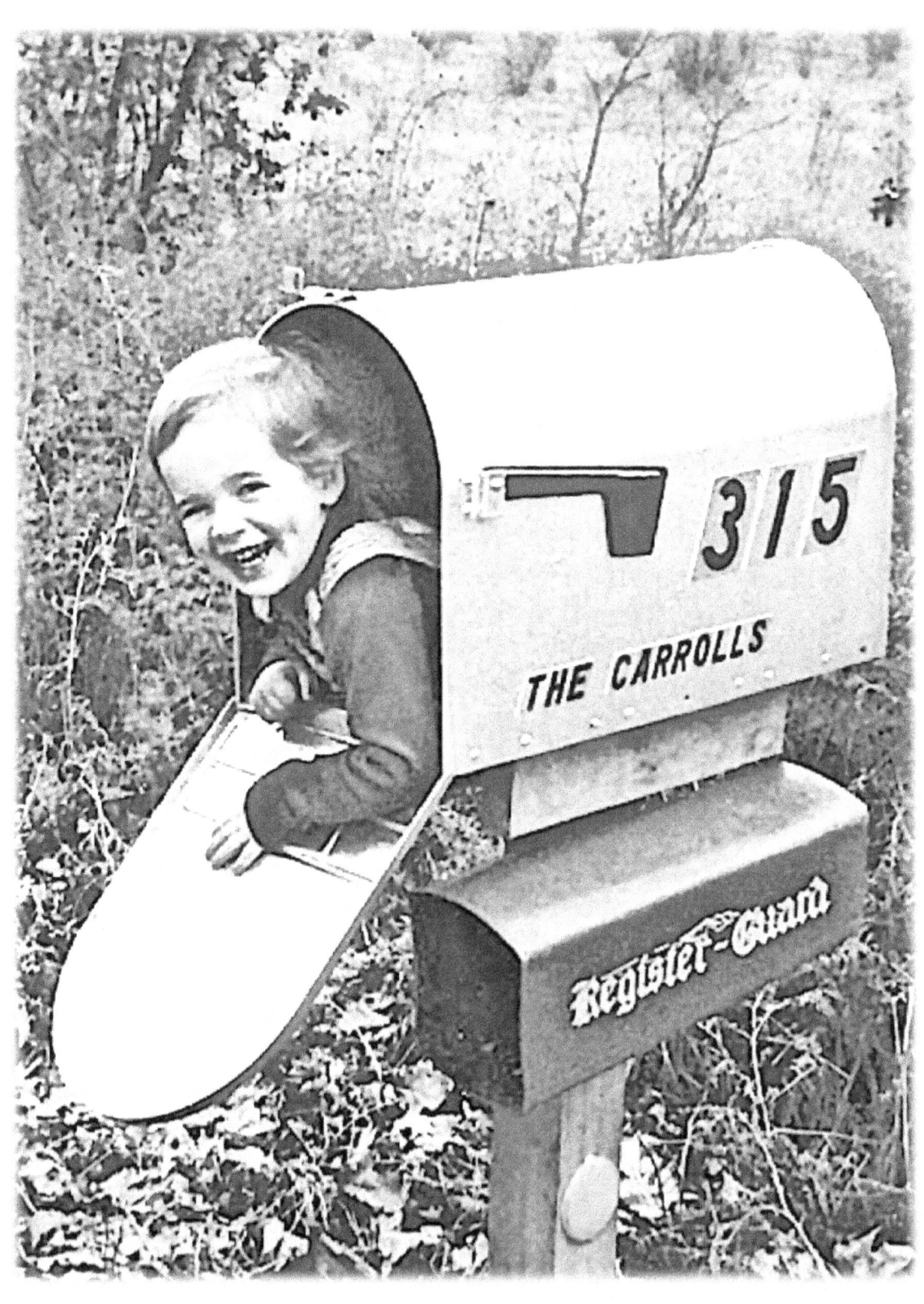

SURPRISE!

SURPRISE!
AMAZON AUTHOR PAGE: www.amazon.com/author/janetlong
ETSY SHOP, "JLA" www.janetlongarts/shop/Etsy.com
ETSY VINTAGE SHOP: www.etsy.com/shop/AdoptionsLtd

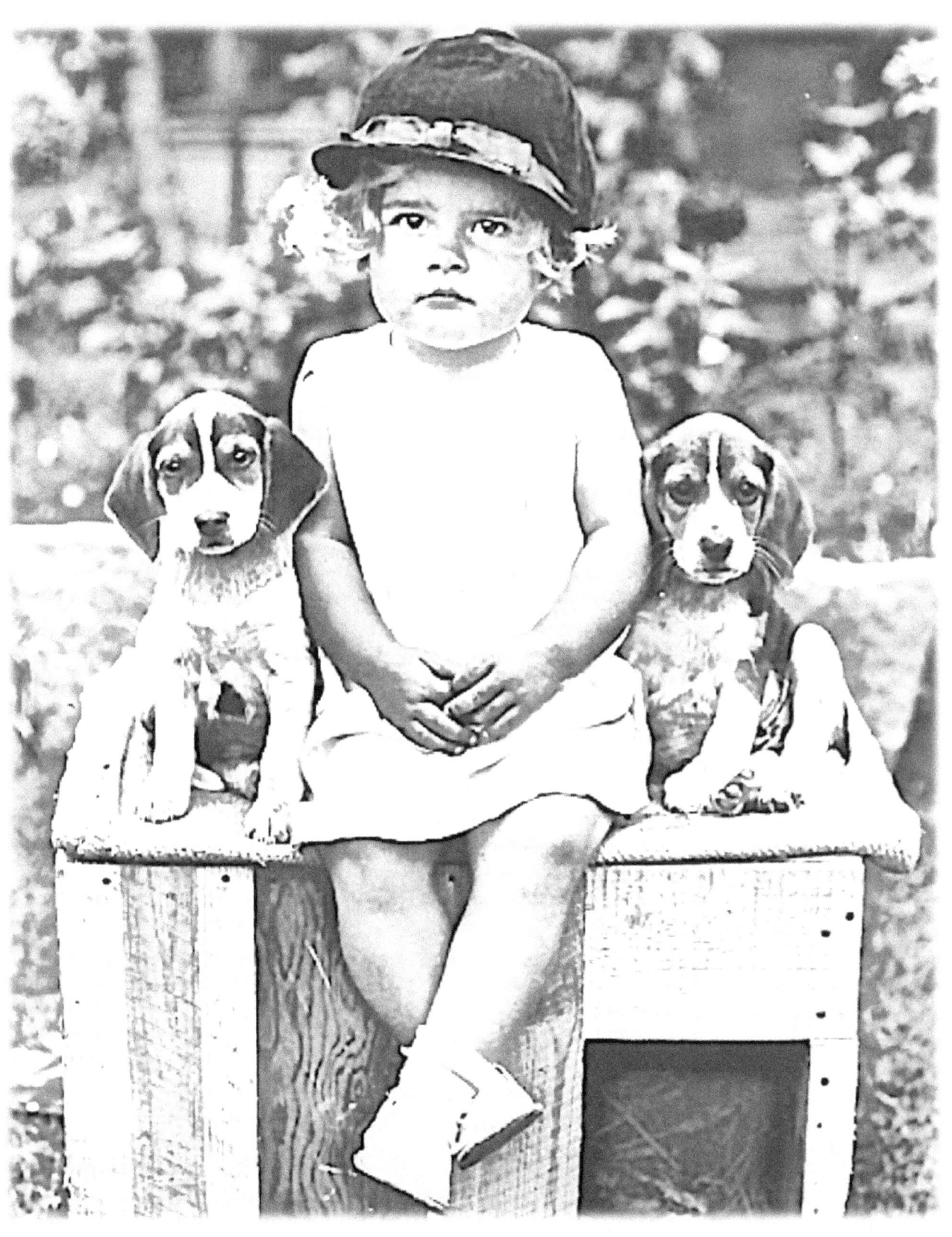

READY for Our CLOSEUPS!!

READY for Our CLOSEUPS!!
AMAZON AUTHOR PAGE: www.amazon.com/author/janetlong
ETSY SHOP, "JLA" www.janetlongarts/shop/Etsy.com
ETSY VINTAGE SHOP: www.etsy.com/shop/AdoptionsLtd

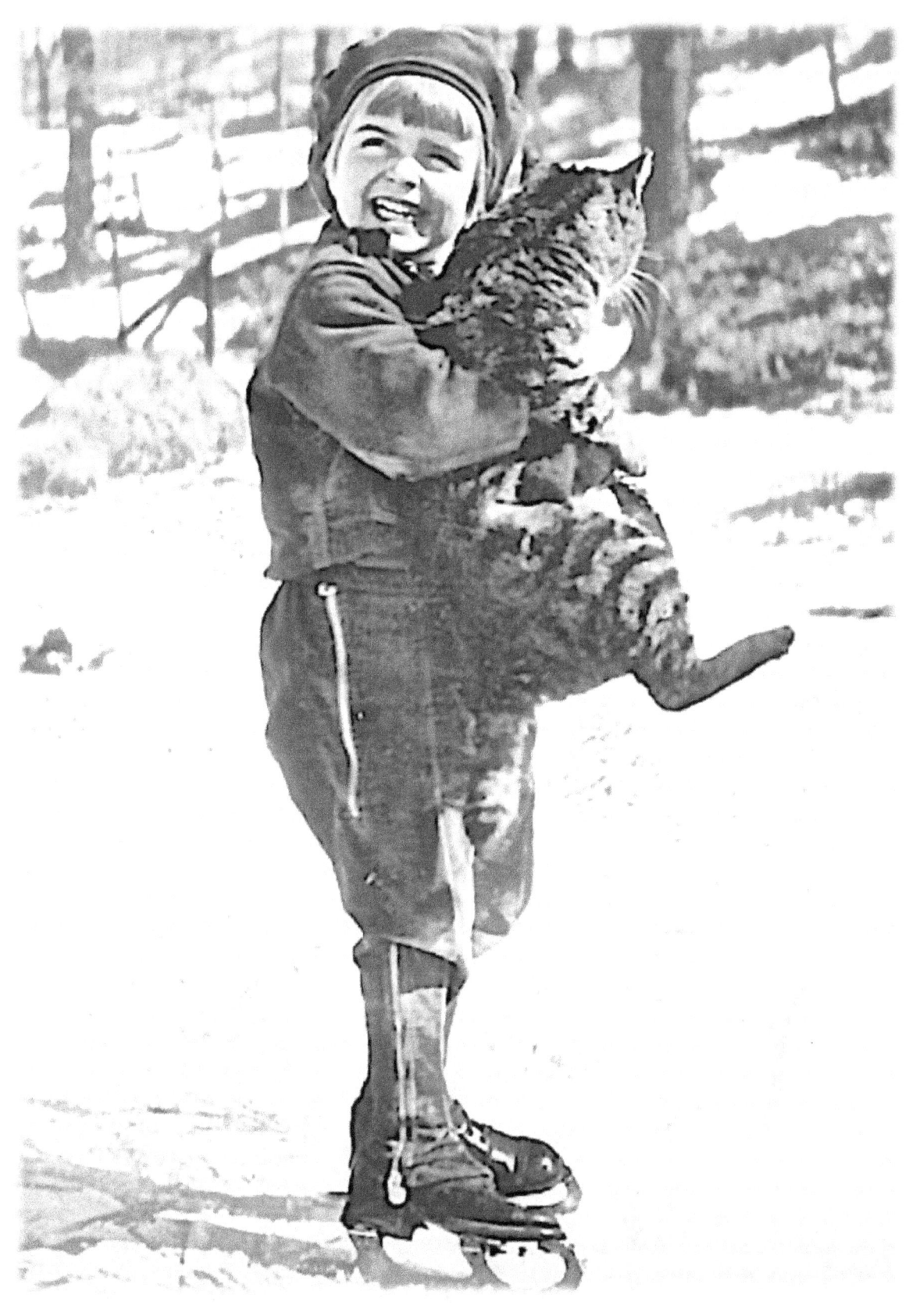

WHAT'D You THINK I'M DOING

I'M TEACHING THE CAT TO SKATE!!
AMAZON AUTHOR PAGE: www.amazon.com/author/janetlong
ETSY SHOP, "JLA" www.janetlongarts/shop/Etsy.com
ETSY VINTAGE SHOP: www.etsy.com/shop/AdoptionsLtd

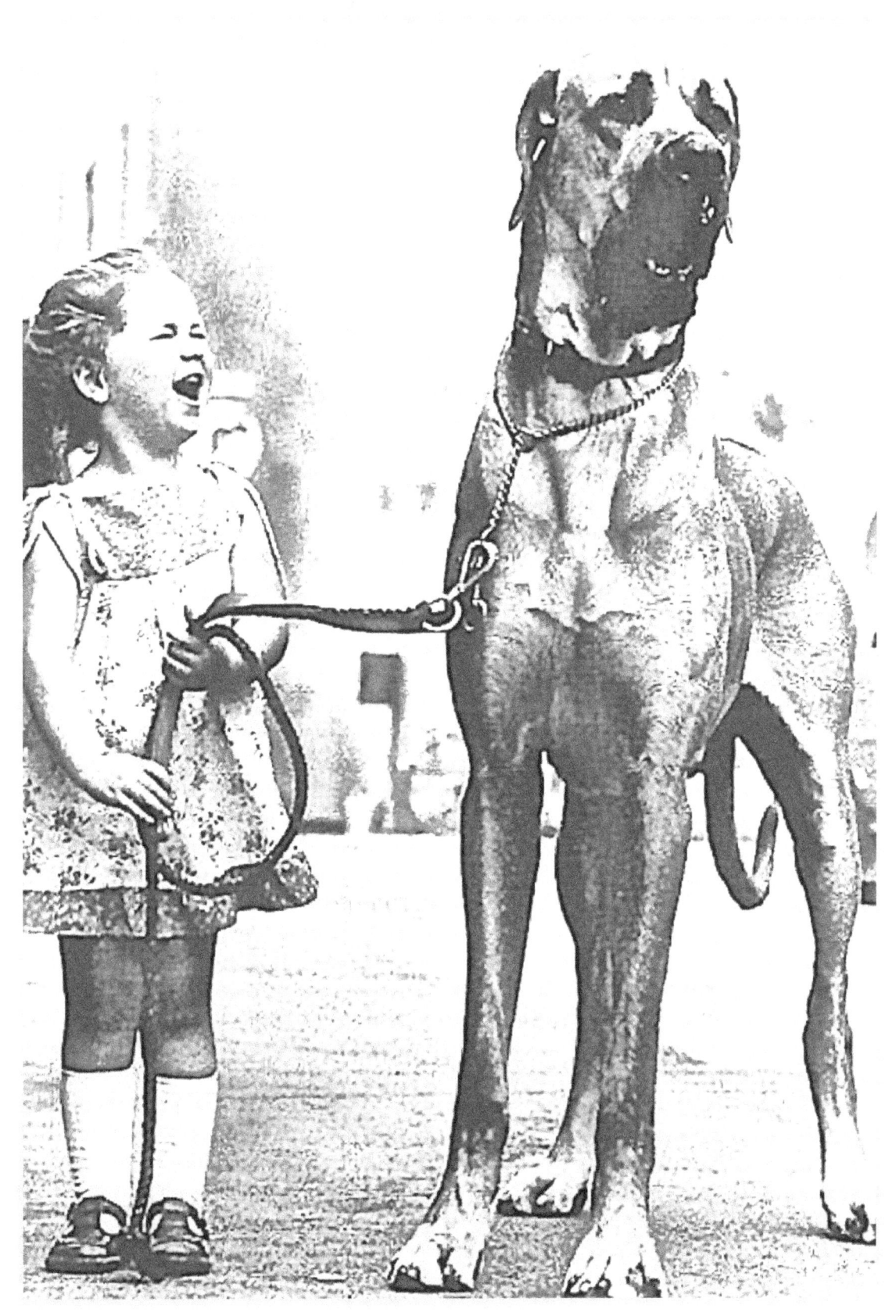

WHOSE MOUTH IS BIGGER?

WHOSE MOUTH IS BIGGER?

AMAZON AUTHOR PAGE: www.amazon.com/author/janetlong
ETSY SHOP, "JLA" www.janetlongarts/shop/Etsy.com
ETSY VINTAGE SHOP: www.etsy.com/shop/AdoptionsLtd

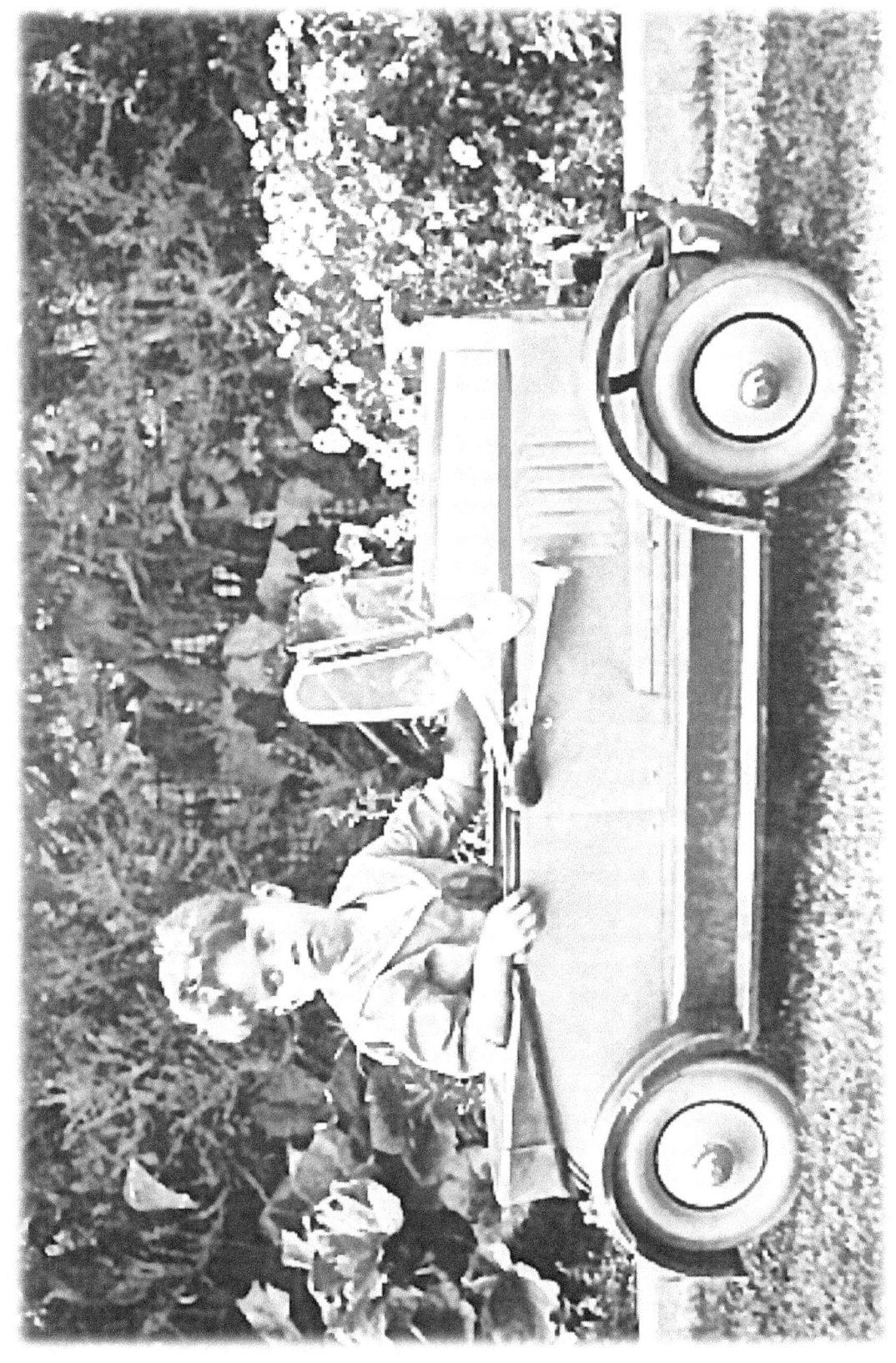

LIKE MY NEW RIDE?

LIKE MY NEW RIDE?
AMAZON AUTHOR PAGE: www.amazon.com/author/janetlong
ETSY SHOP, "JLA" www.janetlongarts/shop/Etsy.com
ETSY VINTAGE SHOP: www.etsy.com/shop/AdoptionsLtd

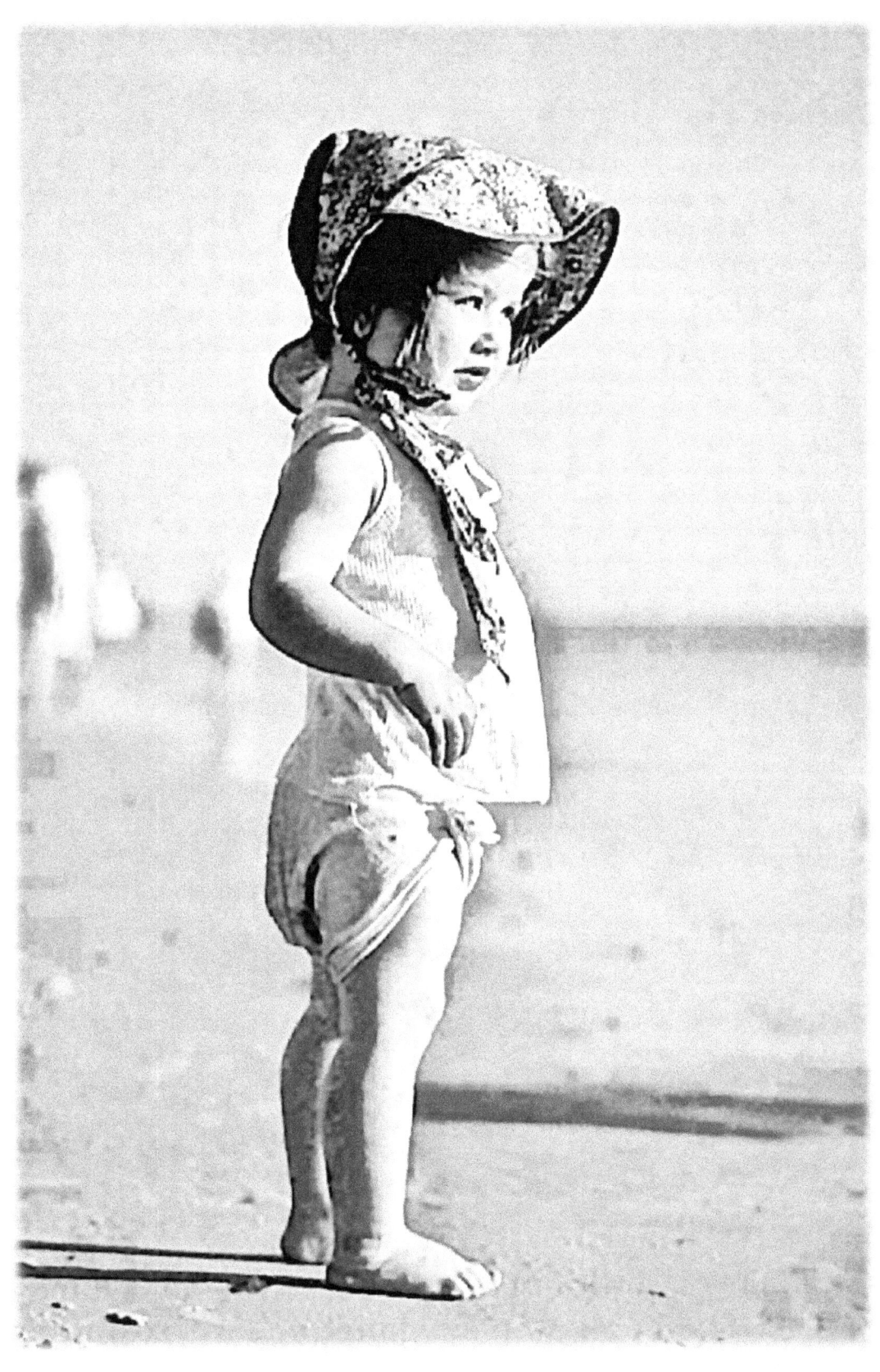

DO WHAT . . . ?

DO WHAT . . . ?

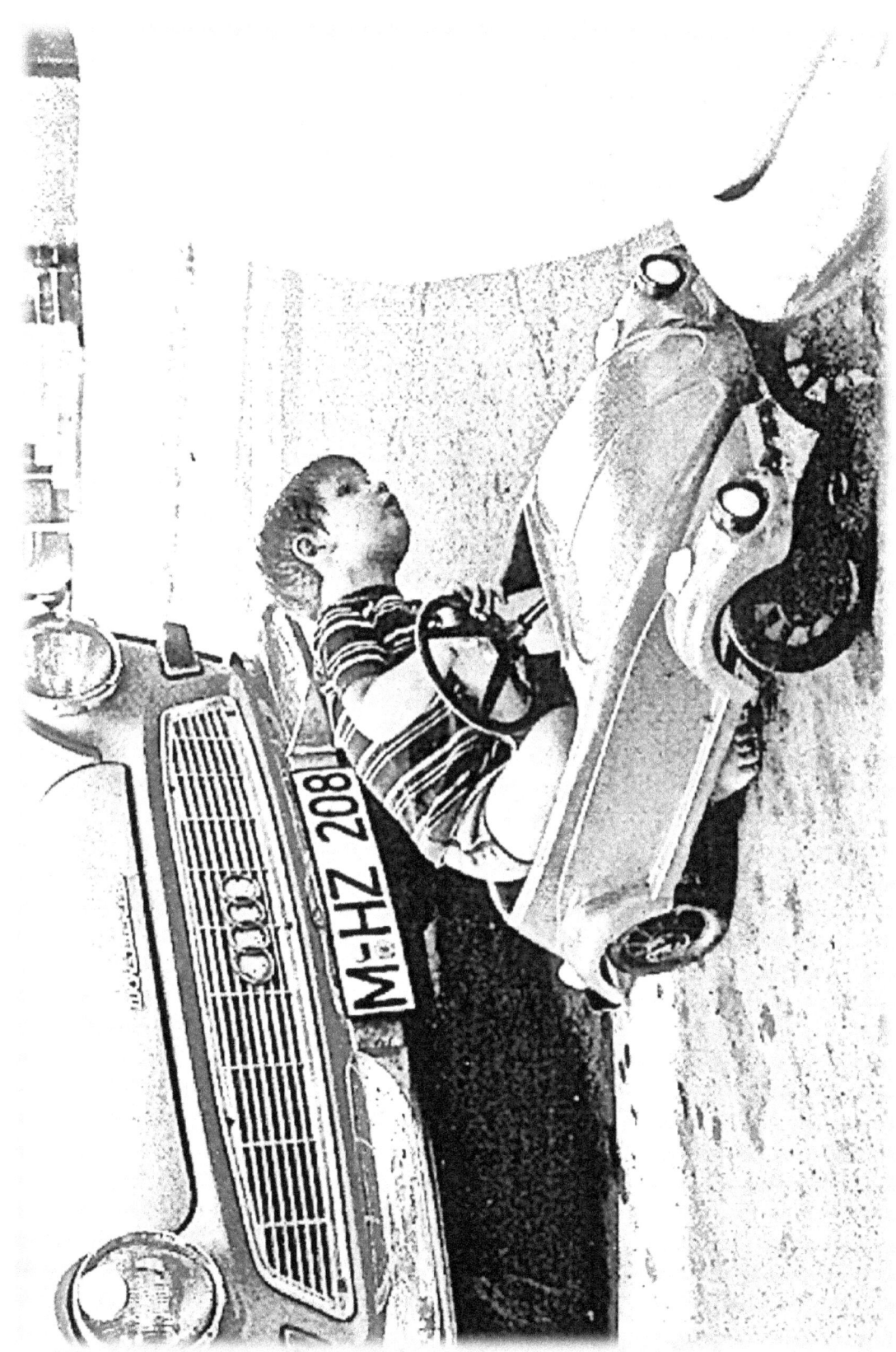

ALMOST THERE!!
AMAZON AUTHOR PAGE: www.amazon.com/author/janetlong
ETSY SHOP, "JLA" www.janetlongarts/shop/Etsy.com
ETSY VINTAGE SHOP: www.etsy.com/shop/AdoptionsLtd

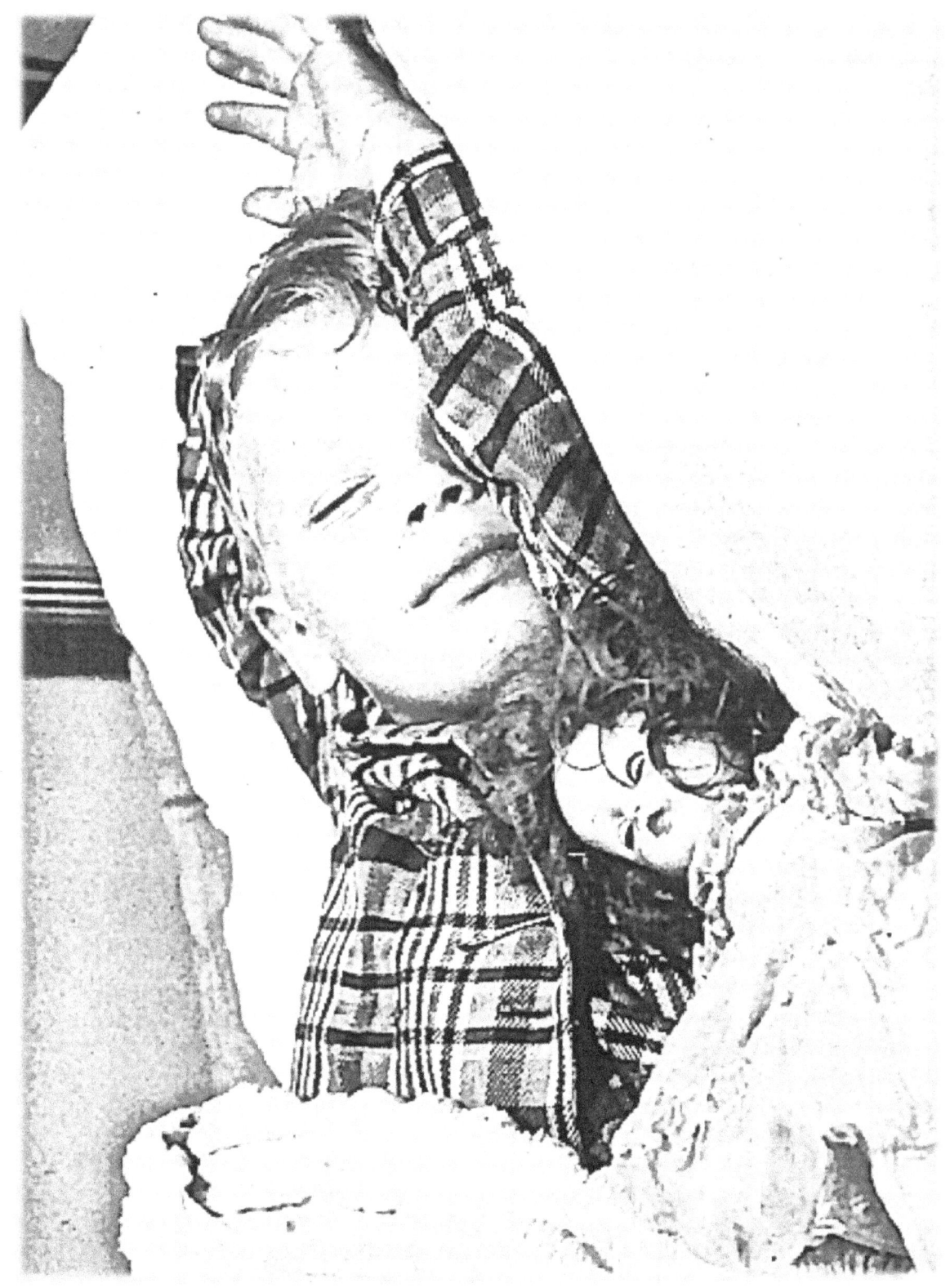

SWEET DREAMS

AMAZON AUTHOR PAGE: www.amazon.com/author/janetlong
ETSY SHOP, "JLA" www.janetlongarts/shop/Etsy.com
ETSY VINTAGE SHOP: www.etsy.com/shop/AdoptionsLtd

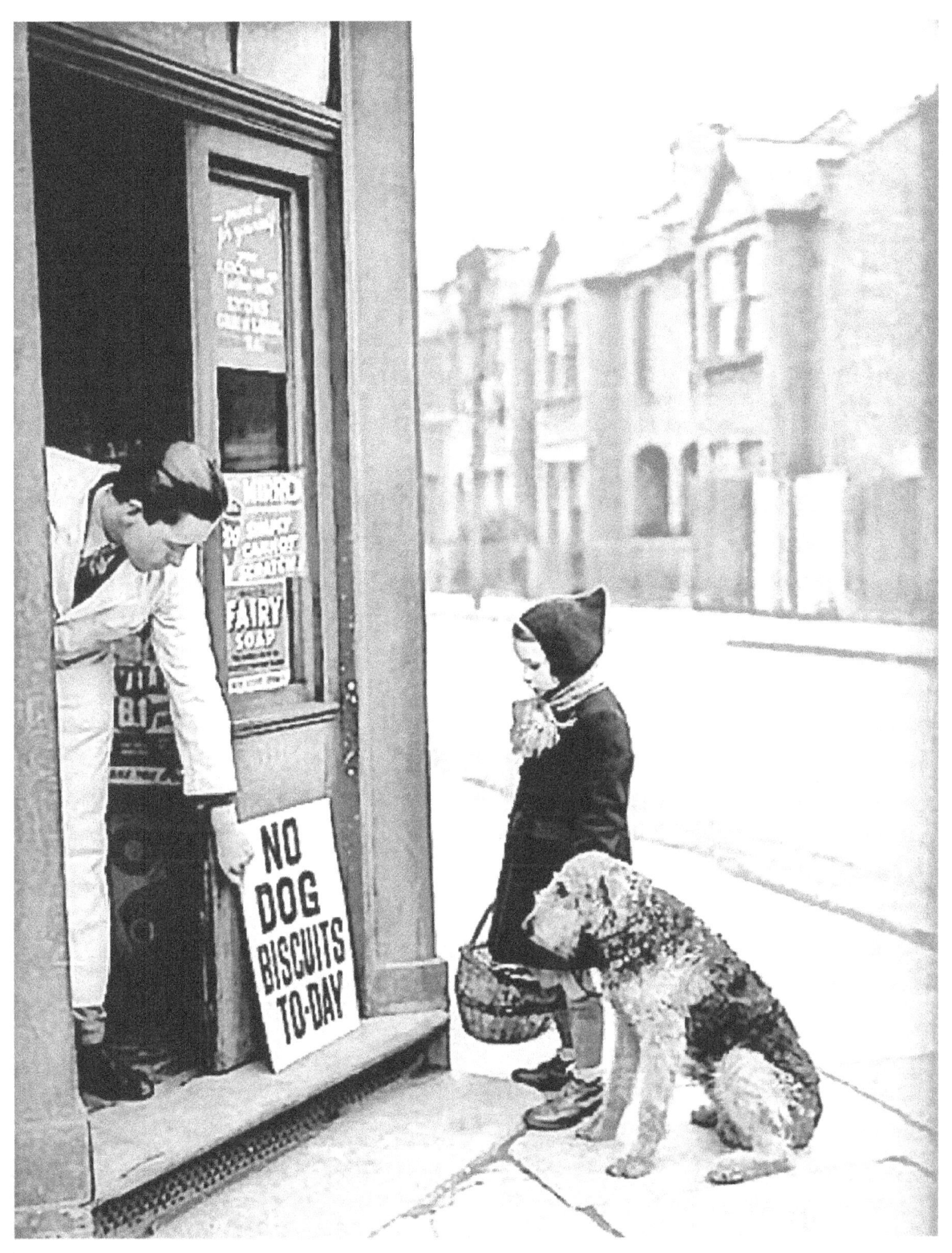

WHY NOT?!

WHY NOT?!
AMAZON AUTHOR PAGE: www.amazon.com/author/janetlong
ETSY SHOP, "JLA" www.janetlongarts/shop/Etsy.com
ETSY VINTAGE SHOP: www.etsy.com/shop/AdoptionsLtd

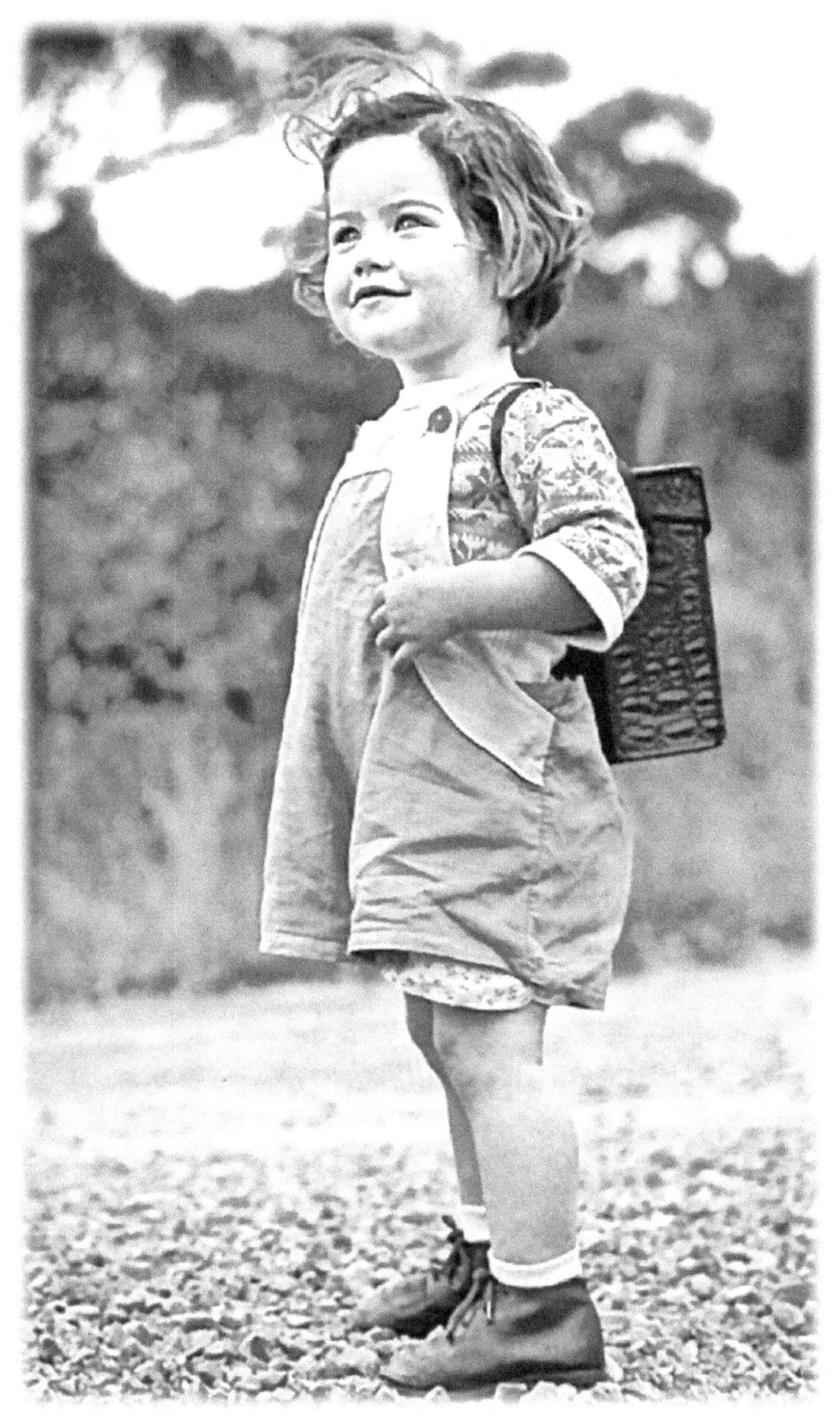

I'M A TROUPER!

I'M A TROUPER!
AMAZON AUTHOR PAGE: www.amazon.com/author/janetlong
ETSY SHOP, "JLA" www.janetlongarts/shop/Etsy.com
ETSY VINTAGE SHOP: www.etsy.com/shop/AdoptionsLtd

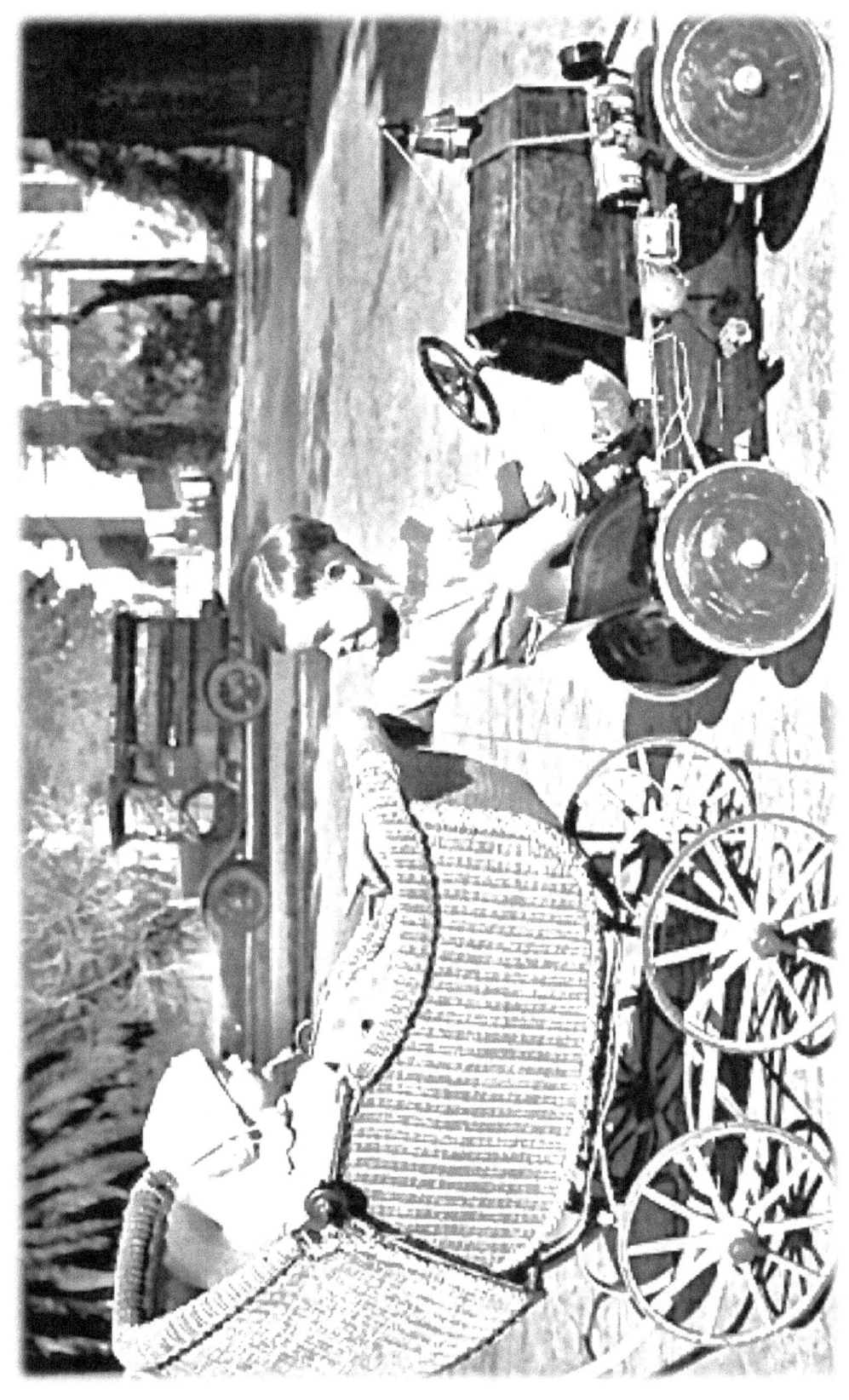

IT'S A PARADE!
AMAZON AUTHOR PAGE: www.amazon.com/author/janetlong
ETSY SHOP, "JLA" www.janetlongarts/shop/Etsy.com
ETSY VINTAGE SHOP: www.etsy.com/shop/AdoptionsLtd

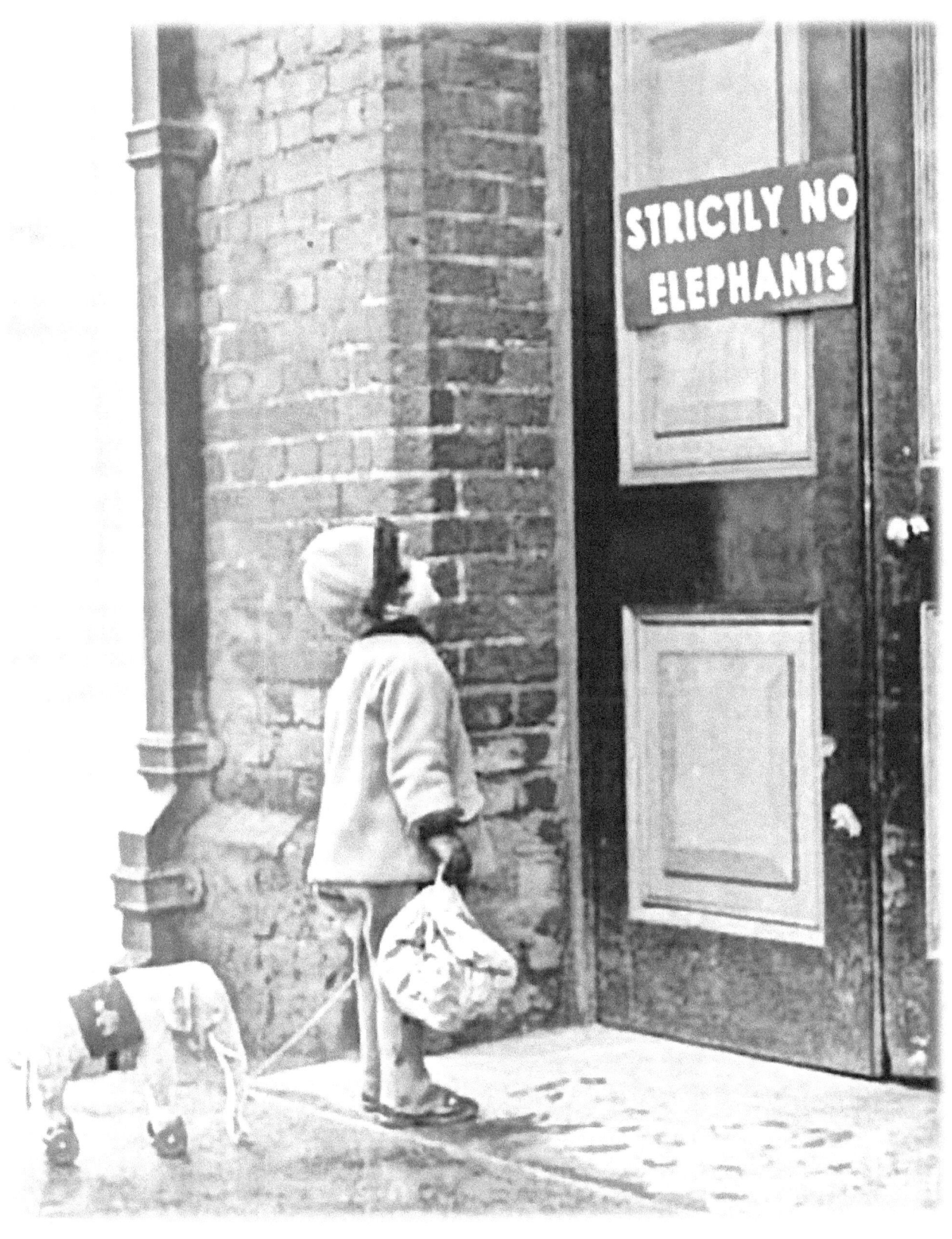

NO ELEPHANTS??!!

NO ELEPHANTS??!!
AMAZON AUTHOR PAGE: www.amazon.com/author/janetlong
ETSY SHOP, "JLA" www.janetlongarts/shop/Etsy.com
ETSY VINTAGE SHOP: www.etsy.com/shop/AdoptionsLtd

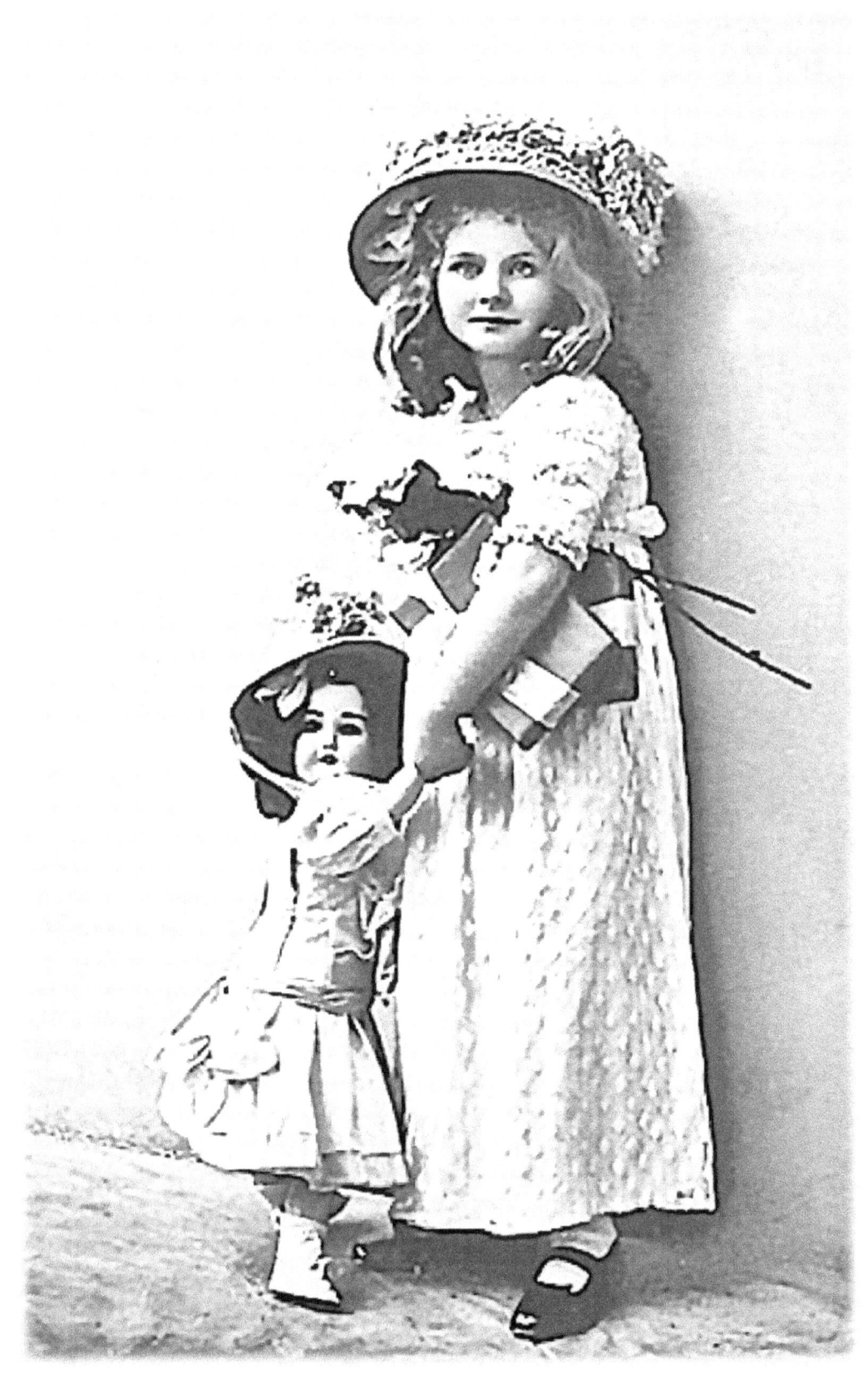

WE'RE TWINS!

WE'RE TWINS!

AMAZON AUTHOR PAGE: www.amazon.com/author/janetlong
ETSY SHOP, "JLA" www.janetlongarts/shop/Etsy.com
ETSY VINTAGE SHOP: www.etsy.com/shop/AdoptionsLtd

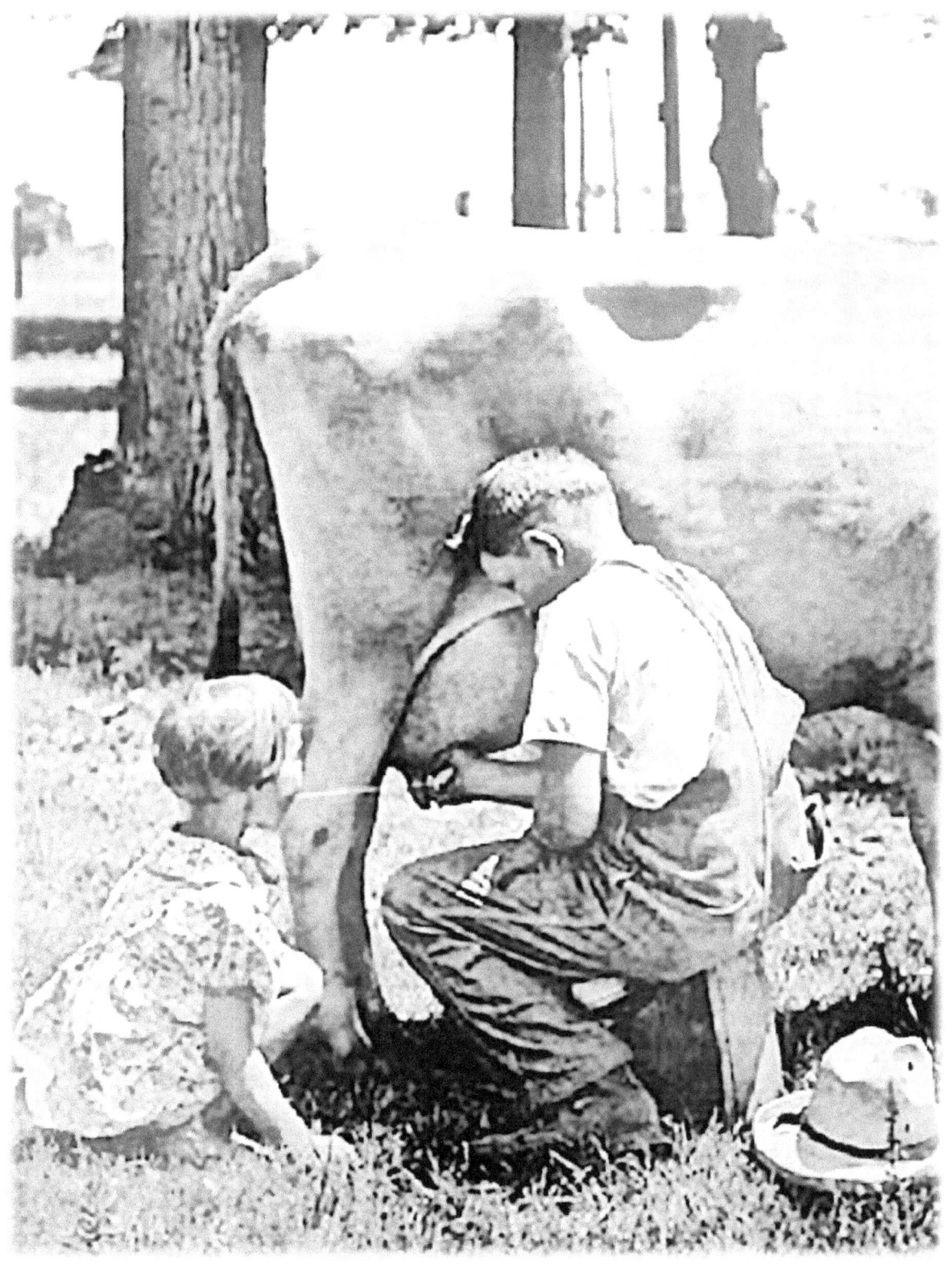

YUM!

YUM!

AMAZON AUTHOR PAGE: www.amazon.com/author/janetlong
ETSY SHOP, "JLA" www.janetlongarts/shop/Etsy.com
ETSY VINTAGE SHOP: www.etsy.com/shop/AdoptionsLtd

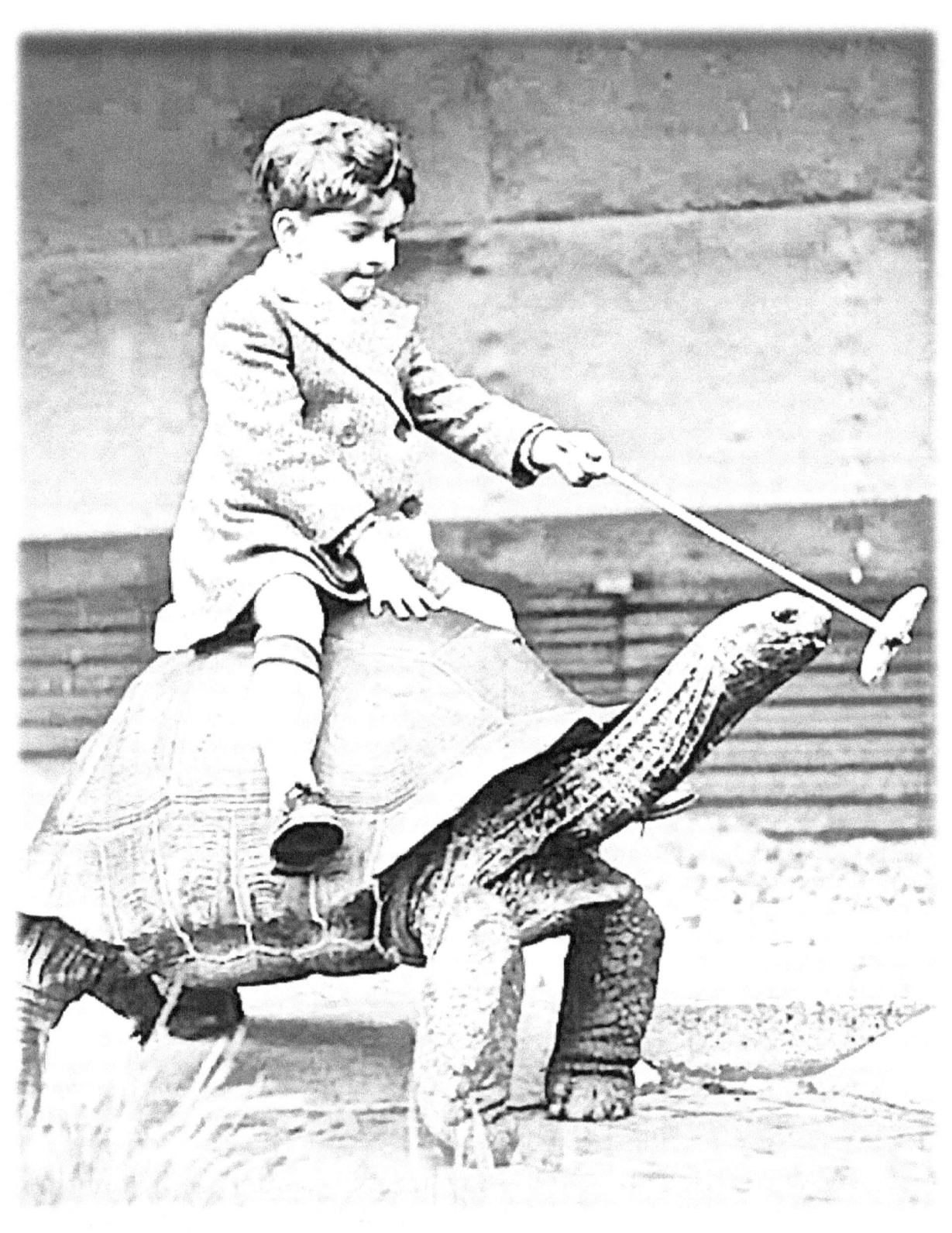

HE LOVES SAUSAGES!

HE LOVES SAUSAGES!
AMAZON AUTHOR PAGE: www.amazon.com/author/janetlong
ETSY SHOP, "JLA" www.janetlongarts/shop/Etsy.com
ETSY VINTAGE SHOP: www.etsy.com/shop/AdoptionsLtd
© 2017 Janet Long Arts. All rights reserved.

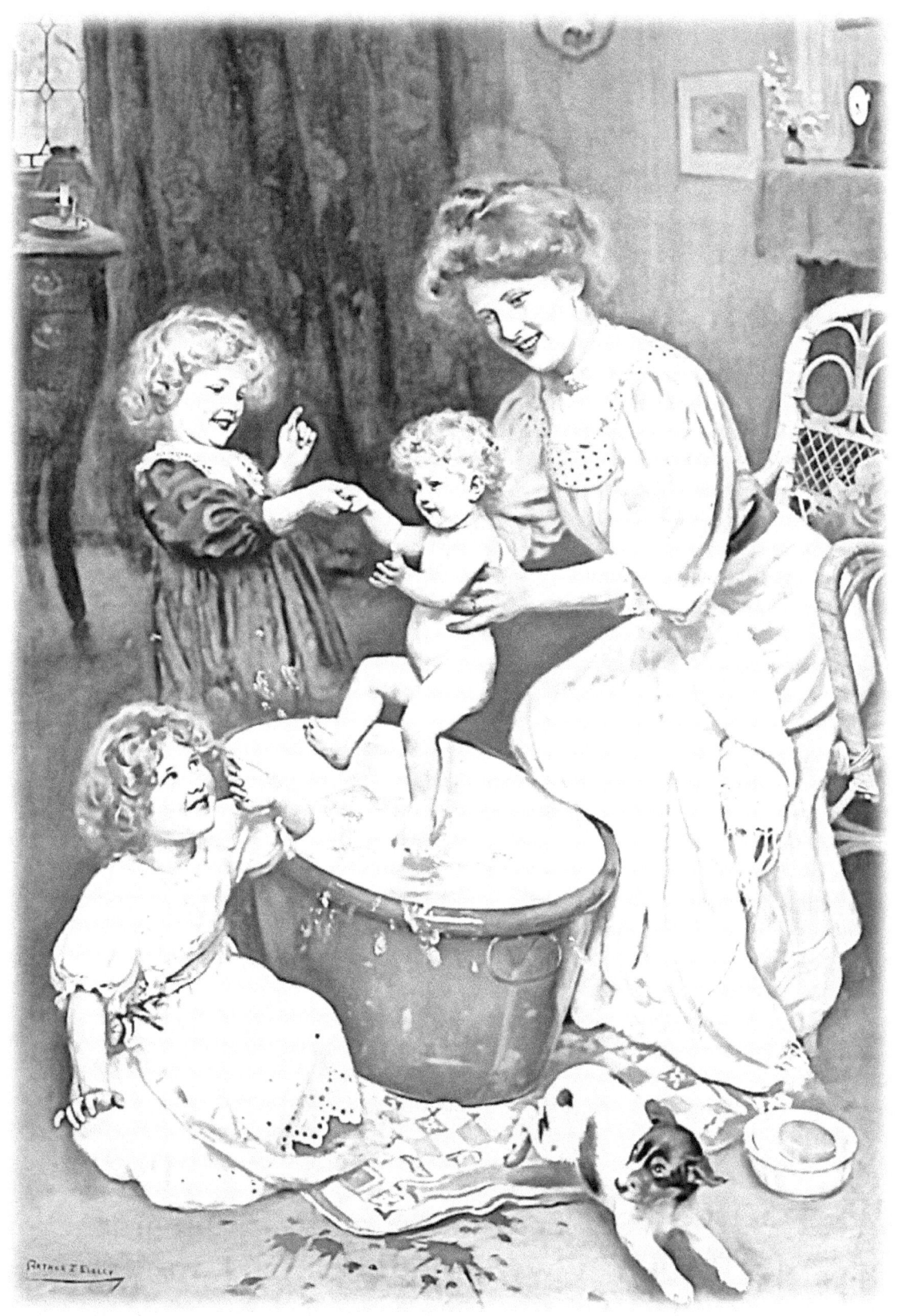

BATHTIME!

BATHTIME!
AMAZON AUTHOR PAGE: www.amazon.com/author/janetlong
ETSY SHOP, "JLA" www.janetlongarts/shop/Etsy.com
ETSY VINTAGE SHOP: www.etsy.com/shop/AdoptionsLtd

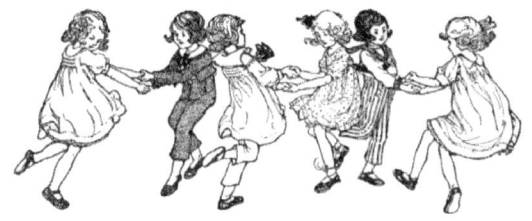

This page is for your notes & coloring tools tests

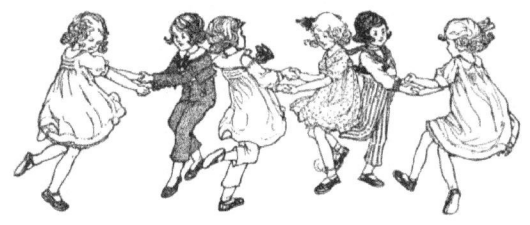

This page is for your notes & coloring tools tests